DEAR MR HOWARD

Michael Wallerstein

MICHAEL WALLERSTEIN was at Downing College, Cambridge, as a student under Dr F. R. Leavis. After teaching English both abroad and in this country, he became a lecturer at a college of education specialising in the primary field. He became interested in linguistics, especially in its educational and social aspects, and gained an M.Ed. from Bristol University, where he was able to develop these interests. Upon taking early retirement, he changed tack entirely and took a science degree in Geology, a subject he had been interested in in his school years. He concluded his academic career, at the age of 60, with an M.A. in Archaeology.

DEAR MR HOWARD

THE CHANGING
OF MODERN ENGLISH

Michael Wallerstein

Edgeways

copyright © The Brynmill Press Ltd 2003

first published 2003
by
Edgeways Books
a division of
The Brynmill Press Ltd
Pockthorpe Cottage, Denton, Harleston
Norfolk IP20 0AS England

printed by Antony Rowe Ltd, 2, Whittle Drive,
Highfield Industrial Estate, Eastbourne, E. Sussex   BN23 6QT

ISBN 0 907839 77 0

www.edgewaysbooks.com

All Brynmill publications are unsubsidized.

DEAR MR HOWARD

DEAR MR HOWARD,

I should like to make a few comments on your piece appearing at the beginning of February 2002 in *The Times*, if you would so allow me.

First, there are some minor points to do with the items you list: you call *enthuse* a solecism inasmuch as it is a back-formation from *enthusiasm*. I cannot see why you so condemn it for, by that account, so must be *opine*, *opt*, *intuit*, *donate* and even *beg* and *burgle*. Back-formations are not essentially different from "forward-formations" (*e.g. enthusiastically*, *opinionated*, *counter-intuitive*, *multi-donational*, *beggarly*); they are derived in conformity with the underlying rules of word-formation in English; indeed, this is one of the principal areas of originality in the language. Furthermore, this sort of word generation cannot be distinguished from "conversions" from one grammatical category to another, wherein English is so rich and which can be so readily accomplished that much of our everyday humour and light intercourse is peppered with them (*e.g. peppered*). They also cause some confusion, of course, when the grammatical category cannot be at once determined—as is sometimes the case in poetry, *e.g.*

I wear-

y of idle a being but by where wars are rife.

and:

Though worlds of wanwood leafmeal lie.

(both G. M. Hopkins)

(What is the category of "but" and "by"? Is
"leafmeal" a noun or an adverb?—the answer, in both
cases, is given by the alliteration, and hence the
rhythm.)

I say "in poetry" but, in point of fact, the confusion
occurs in some common locutions such as "to leave
well alone", where *well* is misidentified as modifying
alone rather than as a noun; again, even clergymen
seem to fail to understand the Lord's Prayer, for one
often hears "Thy will be done" spoken as though *will*
were not a noun but an auxiliary verb to "be done".
These misinterpretations are apparent in the intonation of the speakers.

If a beggar *begs* and a burglar *burgles*, then a pedlar
must *peddle* (it should be *pedle*, but the Americans
reverse the business and have, instead, *peddler*) and
the liar *lie*. Similarly, the braggart must *brag*, the
laggard must *lag* and the coward be *cowed*, the
drunkard must needs *drink*, the dotard no doubt *dote*
and the dullard be *dull*. And why shouldn't the vicar
vick and the bursar *burse*—as well as *reimburse* and
disburse? (Granted, the poor bastard poses a problem.)

It seems to me that the true solecisms lie
elsewhere, and arise from an ignorance of the rules of
the language—not that these need be held in the
consciousness. To add or alter—or, indeed, to
delete—lexical words in a language is not to change it,
for words are easily generated—children do it, as well
as scientists and philosophers (and, contrary to the
vulgar notion, poets, with the exception of Lewis
Carroll, hardly at all). What matters are the
underlying, "invisible", grammatical and semantic
structures. You are indulgent to the use of *like* as a

subordinator (my—American—computer tells me "It looks *like* you are writing a letter"); this seems to me more of a solecism and, indeed, an assault on the language, because it destroys the difference between comparison ("It looks like bad luck") and supposition ("It looks as though it were bad luck"). This indeed leads to a depletion of the resources of the language, and it is this which I believe is actually happening to English. There used to be subtle—but not that subtle—distinctions between:

> It looks like rain (to me).
> It looks as though it's raining (over there).
> It looks as if it were raining (in this photo).

(Note, in addition, the distinction, now obliterated, between *like* and *such as*.)

I offer two recent examples of this development, one from an archaeologist of the Museum of Perth: "It is like they [fossilised animals] went to sleep and their bones are lying in perfect articulation where they died."* (Note the clash of tenses: *went . . . are*.) This is the speech of a, presumably, educated man. Would his written language be much better? (See also the many other examples of the grammar of modern academics scattered through this letter.) And what of this example of spoken English, quoted in *The Daily Telegraph*: "If a friend joined [the FBI] it would be cool. I'd [?It'd] be like, wow he's an agent, and he's a Muslim"?† Of this, more below.

I am not sure but that the above is related to a shift towards *parataxis*. This is where phrases or clauses are set out "end on" without being either conjoined or subordinated. An acquaintance with a public school and Oxbridge education habitually produces such structures as: "apart from it costs too much" and "except

---

* *The Daily Telegraph*, 31.07.02, p. 11   † 31.08.02, p. 17

for it costs too much". This seems to go with an inability to produce reported speech (*oratio obliqua*) so that he says, for instance, "I was wondering will you be going into town?" and, "I told him don't come" and he writes, in a private note: "Say to Mum + Dad about should keep side gate shut." Needless to say, he was awarded a distinction in English Language, including the oral option, and in Literature at "O" Level. I have observed the same phenomena in other "educated" persons of his generation.

Another failure of grammatical comprehension appears in the collapse of distinction between "I doubt he will come" [implying that he will come] and "I doubt whether he will come" [implying that he is unlikely to come]. *Cf.* French: "J'en doute!" and "Je m'en doute!"

The failure lies at the point of SUBORDINATION—and this area, this "hinge" of grammatical structure, will be looked at again in this letter.

Where I think one needs to look for real changes in the language—any language—is in the grammatical and semantic forms, covering not merely the sentence but the whole text, including dialogue structures. If I am greeted, when I enter a shop, whether of the corner or the department kind, an office, either of the local motor mechanics (now, of course, *auto engineers*) or of a solicitor, with "Hi!"—and that only, not as an alternative to any other greeting—then something has happened to the language which both signals and affirms an alteration in human intercourse. (It sometimes gives me mischievous amusement to reply with "How do you do?", which is received either with a blank stare or, after a second's pause, a repetition of "Hi!") If a little study tells one that this greeting originated in the USA amongst adolescents (*teenagers*, now), then its adoption, first by non-American adolescents and then by non-Americans of all ages, also tells one something about the structure of our social life. (The first time I was addressed with "Hi!" was by academic colleagues in 1977.)

The loss of the second person singular, in the eighteenth century, similarly both signalled and sealed an alteration in social relationships: it was the labouring classes who retained it longest, up until the present day in the North, where it was—and still is by some— used in certain intimate social settings, including "flyting". (I was sworn at in the second person singular, the other day, by a not-old van driver.)

This constatation is reinforced by noting the current incidence in this country of the "modern English" locutions in the left-hand column, the traditional British English equivalents of which are given opposite:

M.E.	B.E.
Hello there!	Hallo! / Hullo! / *Sheffieldish:* All right, are you? /
How're you doing?	How do you do? / *Sheffieldish:* How are you going on? /
How may I help you?	Yes? / What is it? / *Sheffieldish:* Now then, Love? [falling intonation]
Pleased to meet you!	How do you do? / I'm delighted to make your acquaintance
Have a nice day!	Jolly good!
Be my guest! (*cf.* Be aware that ... Be sure to do ...)	Yes, do, by all means!
You're welcome!	Not at all! / Not in the least! / Do!

M.E.	B.E.
Bye now	Goodbye / Cheerio / ta-ta (in Sheffield, pronounced /tərɑː/)
Take care!	Bye-bye / Toodle-oo / Mind how you go! [to a child]
Let's go!	Come along, now!
It certainly *is*!	Of *course* it is! / It is indeed! / Isn't it just!
It sure is!	How *right* you are! / Not half! / You're telling me!
There you go! [falling intonation]	There you are! / There we are!
(Well) there you go! [rising]	Such is life! / I knew it!
Wow!	Well, I never (did)! / Good Heavens! / Good Grief!
. . . and whatever	. . . and what not / . . . and what have you
Whatever!	Be that as it may! / What you will!
Sure!	By all means! / Of course! / You're *right*! / Naturally! / Oh, I do hope so!
Me too!	Same here! / So do I!
[I first heard "Me too!" in England from a female colleague in 1977.]	
Me neither!	Same here! / Neither do I!
really, really good	jolly good / not bad at all / *etc.*
really, really hot / sticky / flat / *etc.*	nice / good and hot / sticky / flat / *etc.*
Right!*	I see / Is that the case? / You don't mean it, do you? / Oh dear!

* Once, when I informed a concerned church assistant, of Billy Graham persuasion, of my daughter's serious illness, his reply was, "Right! . . . Right!" [with rising intonation]—the first time I had heard this in such a context. I was quite offended, as though I had been judged to give the correct catechetical answer. This was in 1988.

M.E.	B.E.
That's *right!*	True enough! / You're right! / So do I! / Same here! / So it is!
Great!	Bloody marvellous! (*sarcastic*)
That's great!	Thanks! / Oh, lovely! / That's most kind of you!
That figures!	Wouldn't you just know it!/ It's all of a piece! / Hah!
What's the problem?	What's the matter? / What's up? / What of it?
No problem!	Don't mention it! / Not at all! / Of course! / By all means!
No way!	Don't you believe it! / By no means! / Not (bloody) likely!
C'mon /kmɑ:n/	Oh, come now! / You can't mean it, can you? / Oh, come off it!
Forget it!	Never mind (now)! / Don't give it a thought!
right now	straightaway / at once / just now / this minute
way back	*of time:* long since / long ago *of space:* far back / miles back / right back
like, . . .	as it were / so to speak / in a manner of speaking / as one might say
I guess	I suppose / I daresay / I imagine / I shouldn't wonder
How come (. . .)?	How's that? / How comes it that . . . ? / What makes you say so?

M.E.	B.E.
Why? [rising glide]	Why's that? / Why not? / Why ever not? / What makes you say so?
O.K. [falling intonation]	Very well / I see / Jolly good
... and all that crap	... and so on and so on / ... and all that rubbish
Chris[t]! / Jesus!	Good Lord! / Good Heavens! / Good Grief! / God Allbloodymighty!
Shit!	Damn! / Blast! / Bloody Hell! / What a nuisance!
Bullshit!	Bollocks! / Codswallop! / Balls! / Piffle! / Fiddle-sticks!
He's a real shit.	What an utter cunt/ bastard / bugger he is!

[B.E. = Traditional British English, with various degrees of formality. The computer "spell-checker", which claims to offer U.K. spellings and grammar, underlines *cheerio, ta-ta, toodle-oo, Allbloodymighty, bollocks* and *codswallop* but NOT *bullshit.* No grammatical fault is found with "Me too!" but "Same here!" is questioned.]

I think a comparison of the two sides of the table above demonstrates the relative impoverishment of "Modern English" in conversational interjections and "fillers" by comparison with Traditional British English, not only in diminution of variety but in the absence, in many cases, of internal grammatical structure. This latter point is of enormous significance.

You cite, also, the change from "Have you (got) a . . . ?" to "Do you have a . . . ?" What you don't say is that the former is British and the latter American. I find that even if I pose the question in the British form, the reply I now receive is "Yes/No I/we do/don't." This is of some interest inasmuch as the respondent is replying to something in his/her mind, not mine. I think this, as in the case of *like*, counts as a loss to our linguistic resources. You must know the old joke about two lady passengers on a transatlantic liner, one American the other British, between whom this conversation takes place:

> A: "Do you have any children?"
> B: "Yes, about one a year."

I was once asked: "Do you have any failing students?" What was the answer to this?

Have you ever heard: "Baa Baa, Black sheep, *do* you *have* any wool?"?

The verb *to have* exists in B.E., but not in American English, in three guises: as a "full" verb, where it conjugates in the same paradigm as other main verbs ("Did John have a cold?"), as an auxiliary in the tense patterning of main verbs ("Has John lost his voice?"), and also as a verb somewhat between these two ("Has John a wife and children?"). The construction with *do* ("Does John have tea with his family?") is frequentative. Contrast "Does John have a cold?" with "Does John have a career?" The former is impossible in B.E. because a cold is a visitation not a possession. The Americans cannot grasp this distinction—and I note that my own children seem unable to, either. A further point of some interest is that, in the Yorkshire dialects, not only can the auxiliary be contracted ("You've not got a cold, have you?" *cf.* Standard: "You haven't got a cold, have you?"), but so can the "full" verb ("You've not change for a fiver, have you?" "No, sorry, Love, I've not"). I say this is of interest because it makes explicit my point about the existence of *have* in three semantic/grammatical forms.

May I lay out some other areas of linguistic change that I believe are also of quite serious significance, that is, social and conceptual significance?

The prepositional system is undergoing a wholesale shift. The Americans (and, after a lapse of time, so will the British) replace *of* by *for* in "evidence of . . .", "love of . . .", "proof of . . .", "experience of . . .". (Since beginning this letter, I have received a flyer from a learned society which includes this: "The ancestral Solent River region has been known since the 19th century as a prolific area *for* Palaeolithic artefacts and Pleistocene deposits but had, until the 1990s, been generally neglected *for* [*by* in B.E.] research.")

The American use of *through* is also gaining ground in this country. We now see/hear: "climate change through [B.E. *over*] time"; "Monday through [B.E. *to*] Friday"; "through [B.E. *throughout* or *all through*] September". Again, this marks a, slight but real, reduction of linguistic potential.

On is increasingly substituted for a variety of other prepositions. There used to be a distinction between *in the streets* and *on the streets*, only the latter implying prostitution. A patient was *in* a ward, whilst the houseman might be *on* the same ward. Customers (*i.e.* passengers) are now *on* the train and not *in* it and they go *on* the [*sic*] train instead of *by train* (cf. *by post, by air, by land, by sea*). Tickets are available *on* [at] the door. A barmaid is *on* [behind] the bar. People live *on* [in/at] Hampstead, *etc*. *On* [in] the hope(s) of . . ., *on* [in/of] the order of . . ., to make play *on* [of] the fact that . . ., to set store *on* [by] . . ., to jump *on* [at] the chance, *on* the exam paper, *on* question 3, *on* the team, *on* [at] the weekend, *on* the field (the cow was *in* the field but games took place *on* the field), *on* the carpark, *on* the forecourt, the time *on* [by] the clock; *on* piano, trumpet, drums, *etc*. I have even seen (in an American article) a reference to the Man *on* the Moon where the context implied the Man *in* the Moon.

Consider the following example from *Nature*:

> It turns out that recent [tectonic] flexure models can explain concurrent subsidence *of* some islands and uplift *on* others.*

Is there a meaningful distinction intended between the *of* and the *on*? Science is supposed to be very precise in its language usage but no poet—those airy-fairy creatures—would be content with such inexactitude as this.

What does one say in these contexts if one actually means *on* (*e.g.* "The elephants are on the train")? I suppose one has to waft one's hands about, spluttering the while, "No, I mean ON . . ., you know, . . . ON . . . UP . . ."

(Incidentally, the northern use of *on* ("fed up on it", "what's the use on it?") is not indicative of the same confusion as that above, being the equivalent of the southern *of* in these contexts; *i.e.* it is dialectal and not stylistic.)

Take also what has happened to *round, around* and *about*. (We are on the boundary of preposition and adverb, here.) There used to be a variety of locutions in British English using these words to express various nuances of action or state, *e.g.*

> "He's been right round the world."
> "He's been around in the world!"

---

* *Nature*, 408, 07.12.00, p. 651

"He's been round and about for years."
"He's round about 40, I'd say."
"He turned round and round."
"Turn the car round."

These have all been subsumed by *around*. To turn schools *around*—as one of the new political slogans has it—means, to the English mind, to twist them round and round. (There is an unobserved irony, here!) To be invited to "Come In And Look Around", as the shops now say, would imply an invitation to gawp distractedly. We also find *around* replacing "surrounding", as in "There are rules *around* this matter", and "beside" or "with", as in "She has to be *around* her father all the time." The post-positional locutions ". . . or thereabouts" and ". . . or so" are also assimilated into prepositional *around*. Even traditional idioms are altered to conform, so that one hears "to beat *around* the bush", where the alliteration and therefore the rhythmic emphasis and intonational shape are lost. To say something centres *around* a matter rather than *upon* or *in* a matter seems to me to indicate a lesion in the speaker's grasp of language and meaning. Recently, in *The Sunday Telegraph*, A. N. Wilson wrote of the American cardinals attending a meeting with the Pope as "sitting around". The photograph showed them, in fact, to be sitting *round* the room. Similarly, *The Guardian*, in its "Corrections and Clarifications" section has: "Quaoar . . . we said, was '8,000 miles around'."* *Around* implies (or used to imply) that the 8,000 miles does NOT mean the circumference, as the newspaper claimed. But this, of course, will certainly not be corrected. A character-istic example of what is happening here is this, which would, not so long since, have been described as "sloppy English":

* 10.10.02, p. 25

The Earth has continued to go *around* the Sun and the Sun, perforce, moves *around* the Universe. The same physical laws still govern what happens in and *around* the Earth, although our views of some of the processes . . . have changed.*

These four areas, but more especially the latter two, seem to me a diminution of the resources of the language and, in consequence, a restriction of meaning potential (I know this is a contentious statement).

Phrasal verbs are under attack, especially by journalists and those who wish to appear "cool"—the adjunct being shorn off, as witness the following used in the manner indicated even with omission of the adjunct:

> to fold /up *intransitive* [this was the first to arrive here from the USA, perhaps with the *folding* of *The Daily Herald*.]
> to cool /down *intransitive*
> to level /off *intransitive*
> to spark /off *transitive*
> to flare /up *intransitive*
> to warm /up *intransitive*
> to speed /up *intransitive*
> to build /up *intransitive*
> to topple /over *transitive*
> to seal /over *intransitive*
> to sort /out *transitive*
> to pour /out *transitive*
> to battle /against *transitive*†
> to protest /against *transitive*†
> to trigger /off *transitive*†

TO BATTLE (against): "*Battling* corporate sleaze."‡ Did the editor not notice that "battling" can be read as an adjective? And why not use "fighting"?

* Peter Cattermole, *Building Planet Earth*, 2000, p. vii. *Cf. supra* quotation from *Nature*.
　† See below for examples.
　‡ *The Guardian*, 12.08.02, leading article

"Grants to groups fighting the deportation of asylum-seekers and *battling* the expulsion of disruptive schoolchildren have left the Community Fund embroiled in a bitter row."* All the Brownie-points gained for deleting a supposedly redundant word (*i.e.* against) have been lost by paralleling *fighting* with the synonym *battling* which could, indeed, have been omitted.

TO PROTEST (against): "MPs, race campaigners and victims' groups all *protested* that anyone convicted of a criminal offence should receive a payoff."† This, read in B.E., means that these groups believe that all convicted persons *ought* to have a payoff. This parallels the confusion, also seen in *The Times*, between *protests* [noun] and *protestations* where, in an obituary, someone was described as going on the stage "despite her parents' protestations".

In a recent exhibition about the Holocaust and other genocides, one of the captions read, ". . . they *protested* the charges." Were they for them or against them? (Incidentally, the caption writers also seemed undecided whether refugees were *interred* or *interned*. I tried to draw the attention of the organisers to this, but they appeared perfectly indifferent.)

TO TRIGGER (off): "Water shortages could . . . *trigger* economic stagnation."‡ One supposes, equally, that water shortages may / might / must / will / would / can / could spark / speed / build economic stagnation.

"He believed two soldiers ... were responsible for *triggering* the shooting."§

---

* *The Observer*, 13.10.02, bottom of page 1
† *The Times*, 8.08.02, p. 1, bottom of column 1
‡ John Vidal, *The Guardian* supplement, 22.08.02, p. 6
§ *The Guardian*, 17.10.02, p. 1

These latter two are, perhaps, the most patently risible and mindless examples I have seen, to date; but would either their authors or the authors' editors care? Would such people pay any attention to a George Orwell on language or, indeed, understand him?

This suppression of supposedly redundant adjuncts seems to me to entail a diminution, to put it mildly, of linguistic resource, whereas the contrary tendency, namely, of phrasal extension—another characteristic of American English—is a true enrichment of it:

> to miss out (on)
> to lose out (on)
> to chill out
> to check out
> to meet up (with)*

The modal system is in disarray; any issue of *The Times* will illustrate this—articles have *may, might, could* and even *can* and *able to* in random distribution. One frequently sees articles where *may* in the headline is replaced by *could* in the text—and, less frequently, *vice versa*. And this is so even where a supposedly verbatim report is being presented. The weather forecast, which used to be very precise in the nature of its prophecies, shows this tendency, too. This is quite a serious matter as it fudges the nature of the attitude of the speaker/writer to his/her message— and this, no doubt, is an advantage to the journalist. Note, also, that the negative forms of these are not in symmetry with the positive: the negative of [the journalistic] "There could be a war within months" is

---

* I am less happy about this example as it is, in fact, a conflation of *to meet up* (intransitive) and *to meet with* + noun phrase. *Cf. to get it over with*, a collapsed conflation of *to get it over* and *to have done with it*.

NOT "There couldn't be a war within months." This does mean that the modern reader's ability to understand the modal system as used even by D. H. Lawrence, let alone Jane Austen, George Eliot, Dickens and Henry James, is likely to be blunted, at the least.

In this connexion, notice how the modern form of "Would you like a cup of tea?" has become "Do you want a cup of tea?" That is, the force of *would* is no longer understood. Similarly, "How should I know?" has become, first, "How would I know?" and, then, in the young, "How do I know?" What chance is there for the modern schoolchild (or grown-up) to understand the folk-song refrain?—

> Oh that I were where I would be
> Then should I be where I am not
> Here am I where I must be
> Go where I would I cannot

(The computer, tellingly enough, informs me that the *were* in the first line is ungrammatical.)

The fossilised grammar of the phrase *as it were* also now seems to be misunderstood. Jay Parini, poet, novelist, biographer and Professor of English in Vermont, writes, in his biography of Robert Frost:

> When asked if he had any message to deliver to President Kennedy, Frost acknowledged that he did [*i.e.* had]. . . . *As it were*, Kennedy never called [*i.e.* rang] or even sent a note to thank Frost for his efforts, and Frost was deeply hurt".*

Parini seems to think the phrase is the equivalent of *in the event*. One notes, also, the repetition of *Frost* within the same short sentence (*vide* remarks on *style*, below).

* pp. 434–5

The understanding of *must* also belongs in the area of modality. I think you will find that those below the age of about 40 very rarely use this form, and certainly not in the negative (*mustn't*); the expression "You must be joking!" has become "You're joking!" The new Bishop of Bath was recently reported as saying that the price of milk being lower than that of bottled water "has to be wrong." But the point is that it is lower. He, presumably, meant that this *must* be wrong and *has* to be altered.

The removal of *shall* from the system is also part of the trend; even in the interrogative, again following American precedent, one now sees in Social Services information leaflets "When *will* I receive my pension?" Newspapers invariably expand the spoken contracted forms "I'll" and "we'll" to "I will" and "We will", never to "shall". The—formerly—typical dialogue invitation "Shall we go out, this afternoon?" (and in the North, be it noted, "Shall you have a cup of tea?") is replaced by "Do you want to go out . . . ?" and "Do you want a . . . ?"

Incidentally, the future tense, in conversational speech if not in written language, is now almost invariably realised with *BE* + *going to*; this elides any possible distinction between *shall* and *will* (*e.g.* "I'm going to go to bed early, tonight.")

That *will* and *shall* are part of the modal system is demonstrated by trying the effect of swapping one for the other, *e.g.* "Thou *wilt* not commit adultery" (if this were so, one would not have to try!); "You *shall* always be right, *shan't* you!" (it would be nice to think one could be!); Shylock says, of his pound of flesh: "'Tis mine and I *will* have it!" That is, he means to have it now, not in the future (*shall*). Could President Bush, or any other American president since the time of, say, Theodore Roosevelt, make anything of this, formerly obvious, distinction?

The modal verbs are part of the larger system which includes the modalities ("moods" of traditional grammar) of the exclamatory and the emphatic. These, also, have become near-defunct; that is, their realisation in the grammar and syntax. Consider these examples of—formerly—very ordinary, every-day speech:

> X: "Oh, how *lovely* she looked! Y: "Yes, *didn't* she just!"
> X: "What a *wonderful* day it was, *wasn't* it!"
> Z: "Oh, you *are* kind! / Oh, how *kind* of you!"

The present realisation of these utterances is likely to be:

> X: "She looked really, really nice (yeah?)"
> Y: "(Yeah) I agree / really nice (yeah)."
> X: "It was a great day, right?"
> Z: "That's really, really kind of you!"

The highlighting of elements by means of voice tone has diminished enormously. Attend a dramatic performance given by students and their inability to do this is quite striking—and distressing. The tonic accent tends to be shifted always to the final word in the clause, regardless of meaning. But observe, also, the syntactical impoverishment of the modern forms—the absence of inversion and the absence of tag questions. (All tag questions are replaced, now, by "yeah?" or "right?" or "innit?". It might be claimed that these are no worse than the general purpose *n'est-ce pas?* of French, but the difference, here, is that the former lack internal grammatical structure; that is, they are pidginisations.)

Besides the reduction in the modal system, there is also apparent a reduction in the tense system, where there is a tendency for all the past tenses—even the past continuous (the imperfect) and the past perfect (the pluperfect)—to be collapsed into the simple past (the preterite). This appears, in speech, in everyday utterances such as: "He just arrived", "They just called", *etc*. In B.E., these mean that the subject persons did nothing else beyond arriving and calling. The auxiliary *have* has been suppressed, first in phonic represent-ation and then in conception. I remember an advertise-ment from American magazines of the '50s which read: "Who just called Swan?" (*i.e.* "Who [is it] has just rung up Swan's?") At that time, this was quite unintelligible to me, and it is a further index of our culture that this advertisement is now seen here and raises no queries. Similarly, an anti-speeding notice has recently appeared in our local surgery which reads: "Classroom sizes just got smaller." In B.E., this means that, at some unspecified period in the past, classroom sizes simply got smaller—when this was and why we should need to know this, we cannot tell. We have to "re-write" the sentence to make it yield the intended meaning.

The following is an example from *The Observer*:

> Some £9bn [*i.e.* American billion, presumably] of public money was ringfenced for Network Rail, Railtrack's not-for-dividend successor, as working capital. But in recent months another £6bn was needed.*

This is a complete paragraph. If the first *was* is simple past, then so must the second one be, one supposes; but there is a semantic clash between this *was* and "in recent months" because the recent months are, necessarily, still with us and the needful tense is the

---

* 08.12.02, Business Section, p. 7

present perfect. The article has at least a dozen further Americanisms besides the use of the American billion (one thousand million, rather than one million million), which is not made explicit.

A front page of the G2 section of *The Guardian* reads: "How the mobile changed the world."* This implies, in B.E., that the change took place some time since and that it is, in some way, a thing of the past. But we know, from the accompanying picture of an Indian Saddhu holding a mobile 'phone, that the time referred to is, in fact, the present; this understanding is therefore gained NON-LINGUISTICALLY—which is the very point I am making. (Compare, for instance: "How the Black Death changed the world".) How, nowadays, could one say—and mean—"How the mobile changed the world"? We have been robbed of the possibility, except by adding specifying adjuncts—or explanatory pictures.

This collapse of the present perfect into the simple past (*le passé défini*) is, in my view, a huge and irrecoverable loss to the language.

Again, even the "educated" now seem to have difficulty in maintaining a consistent time/tense perspective throughout a sentence which has any sort of subordination. This is especially apparent where the subordinate clause is conditional or concessive. An example from *The Daily Telegraph*: "A huge asteroid is scheduled [!] to crash into the Earth, astronomers announced yesterday. If it *does* it *would* wipe out . . . ."†

A further example, from a letter to *The Times*: "Sir, I may only be a jobbing accountant but I *thought* that gifts to staff, which are convertible into cash, *are* accessible to tax as benefits in kind."‡ This failure of temporal perspective is closely related to the confusion in the modal system described above.

---

* 15.11.02   †25.07.02, p. 1   ‡ 06.12.02, p. 25

I believe these linguistic/conceptual failures (for I think that is what they are) have quite dangerous implications in the realm of both internal and international affairs. I think it might merit a study to look at the contrast between, say, French and English cognition in this area, for French does not admit the present tense after either *si* or *quand* where conceptual speculation or supposition are in question.

The nominal system is also undergoing a radical simplification; traditionally (*i.e.* over the course of centuries), common nouns have tended to fall into two major grammatical categories: "mass" nouns and "count" nouns. *Bread, sugar, tea, coffee, soap, water, air, food, fruit, corn, wheat, oats, shit, timber* and all "abstract" (*i.e.* conceptual) nouns (*honour, humility, greed, psychology, imagination, destruction, impact, number, English, physics, mathematics,* etc.) are mass/uncountable; they cannot take the indefinite article unless qualified (*e.g.* "an unusual imagination"), nor can they be pluralised. But now it is quite common to see, in shops, "All our foods / breads / soaps / beers / jams are made with . . .". "A tea" used to mean a set tea (scones and jam, *etc.* . . . do you remember?); now it just means one cup or pot. Some nouns exist(ed) in both count and mass form, e.g. *fruit,* with different meanings. The fruits of a man's labours are not fruit (ditto *labour!*) In the sentences: "Will you do the honours?" and "It's an honour to me!", the pluralising and the indefinite article demonstrate that, here, the *honour* in question must be different to the uncountable *honour.* That is, the grammar has a clear semantic function (*contra*, for instance, *me* v. *I* or *who* v. *whom*). "In the beginning was the Word [NOT *a* Word OR *the* Word*s*]". I take up this issue, again, below.

Majority could only be used to determine a plural count noun: "the majority of the apples / houses / contestants / voters, *etc.* Now, we see (and hear) "the majority of the food / the river / the blood". An example comes to hand from the *Friends of the Earth* magazine: ". . . the majority of timber sent to Barings' pulp mill . . . has been clear cut from Indonesian rainforest."* (The grammar, here, puts me in mind of the letters I receive from friends in the Far East.) The last census paper asked us to list members of our households who were resident "the majority of time" (note, not even "*the* time"—was it composed by an Asian?). I wrote to the Registrar General about this and received no reply. (The construction with the indefinite article ["a majority of people said . . ."] is the result of careless thinking rather than of grammatical failure.)

Connected with this is a tendency to construe invariable plurals as count plurals; thus we now find: "In the *interest* of hygiene" (hygiene hasn't got any interest in the matter), "*Greeting* cards" (cards don't greet), "On the *ground* that he was absent" (he wasn't on the ground), "*Sport* car, socks, etc." (*sports* is a collective word). Presumably, we shall soon adopt the USA form *math* for *mathematics*, even though the *ics* element is no more plural here than it is in physics, linguistics, gymnastics, *etc.* "Maths *is* [not *are*] my worst subject." There is a brand of sports clothing emblazoned *Russell Athletic*—a Gallicism, perhaps, with post-positional adjective; but one suspects the designers themselves don't know, having lost their sense of what is English.

Abstract/generalising nouns are treated as count-ables, and so we read, and hear, of the *impacts* (no

* Issue 52, p. 7

mere "effect") of global warming and *linkages* between all manner of entities: "Individual sessions will explicitly address the *linkages* between the oceanic and terrestrial records of change."*

However, we have yet to learn of *drainages, postages* or *sewerages*. (The computer, symptomatically, doesn't like the last three but finds no fault with the earlier two.)

This growing confusion of categories is shown up in a neat and instructive way by the labelling on cheap paint-brushes hailing from China; these are stamped with the cachet "PURE BRISTLES". They are made with horse hairs. Good quality paint-brushes are made with hogs' bristles—hence the justified claim of "PURE BRISTLE". This is another example of commerce exploiting and intensifying, consciously or otherwise, the present insecurity of linguistic categories.

Overlapping the count/mass noun contrast is (was) a system distinguishing the inanimate from the animate, the latter itself being subdivided into the human and the non-human. This was reflected and embodied in the relative pronouns: "The man *who* spoke to me / to *whom* I spoke / *whose* speech I heard", "The cow *which* chased me / from *which* we receive milk", "The house *that* Jack built" (The cow might also be *that* but certainly not *who*.) It was dialectal / vulgar to say "the man that" and anyone saying "the cow who" would have been suspected of an unnatural relationship with it (or his lady-friend). But in *The Times*, we read of "the locusts *who* ..." and "the politicians *that* ...". (From a Reuters report in *The Times*: "Oslo: Three polar bears *who* broke into cottages were shot dead by police."† From *Grapevine*:

---

* Circular of the *Quaternary Research Association*, November 2002
† 23.03.02

"... a female king snake *who* could not lay her last egg."*) There is an American children's picture book entitled *The Cow Who Fell In The Canal* (note the capitalisation), by Peter Spier. In the 1970s, I took it that the *who* was a deliberate piece of anthropomorphism. Now, I think I was wrong. There is a (repeated) "Horizon" television programme on the dinosaurs of South America which consistently honours them with the *who* relative; one cannot tell whether their enhanced status is intended or not. Are we supposed to feel more warmly towards them as we would to our pets?

Would one repose any faith in the critical acumen of a writer who can produce this?—

> As a novelist, I appreciated the solicitation of certain publishers *that* went out of their way . . . to draw our attention to novels they were unable . . . to submit for the prize. That showed positive support for their authors. They were doing their job. Compare that to the publisher *that* submitted a novel in manuscript by a former Booker winner, with 18 non-consecutive pages missing.†

In addition to the application of *that* to a human agent is the jarring cacophony of the piece. Would Mr Jones, one wonders, know how to respond to this passage; would he notice the (subtle?) way in which the snake is turned into a companion for the forsaken child?:

> But no one came, and as she lay waiting the house seemed to grow more and more silent. She heard something rustling on the matting; and when she looked down she saw a little snake gliding

---

* August 2002, p. 19

† Russell Celyn Jones, Booker Prize Judge, in *The Guardian*, 22.10.02, p. 19

along and watching her with eyes like jewels. She was not frightened because he was a harmless little thing who would not hurt her, and he seemed in a hurry to get out of the room. He slipped under the door as she watched him.

"How queer and quiet it is," she said. "It sounds as if there was no one in the bungalow but me and the snake."*

This conceptual distinction was also reflected—and maintained—in the lexis: one could both *harm* and *hurt* an animal; but one could not *hurt* a business or a tree. One's pride or conscience could be *hurt*, but when they were *harmed*, this was quite another and much more serious thing. One could *harm* a child very much without necessarily *hurting* him or her in the least. An example from *The Times*: "Police [N.B. not "*the* police"] will be given new powers to arrest internet paedophiles before they can *hurt* children."† But what of the *harm* they, and all pornographers, do not only to children but to society and to themselves, too? That the Americans (for, it is they who cannot see these distinctions) use these words inter-changeably (and *who, which* and *that*) and that we, here, then proceed to copy them, does, I think, tell us something about where our sense of the world is coming from.

(Aside: the fact that, in the 16th and 17th centuries, various mercantile practices were declared by the government to "hurte this owr realme" is beside the point, which is that a distinction between *hurt* and *harm* had been developed over the centuries since

---

* Frances Hodgson Burnett, *The Secret Garden*, 1911 & 1988, p. 10. (Frances Hodgson Burnett was, by origin, American and there are, in fact, quite a number of Americanisms in the novel but this is not one of them.)

† 10.08.02, p. 1, column 1

then. Similarly, the relative pronouns of The Lord's Prayer were modified over the centuries succeeding Wycliffe's 14th-century rendering.)

Again, take the verbs: *raise, rear, bring up.* There was a clear distinction in British English between *raising* crops (inanimate), *rearing* animals (animate non-human) and *bringing up* children (animate human). The idea of *raising* a child was laughable—indeed it was a standing joke derived from Westerns: "Where was you raised?" which went alongside: "a low-down bum". When *child-rearing* (thanks to Dr Benjamin Spock) came to these shores, it at first evoked images of children in cattle-stalls. Is it altogether insignificant to note that Earl Spencer, the South African, speaks of his sister, Diana, as being *raised* and of his public standing being *hurt*?

Another grammatical point related to this division is (was) that, in principle, only personal proper nouns, personal titles and human agents (or specific referents in the speaker's immediate environment, *e.g.* "*my* dog's left ear", "*the* mouse's cage" as against "the left ear of *a* dog", "*a* mouse cage") could take the genitive case: John's hat; Mary's house; the King's Majesty; their Lordships' pleasure; women's lot; a farmer's life.

(Constructions such as: "a hair's breadth", "the river's edge", "my wits' end", "a dog's life" are formulaic; that is, they are non-generative.) But we now have: London's East End; Paris's Eiffel Tower; Naples's Bay; the church's spire; the house's roof; *etc.* These constructions *were* possible, formerly, in a contrastive sense; that is, they were special cases—Naples' Bay as opposed to Naples' mountains; Paris's Eiffel Tower as opposed to Timbuctu's Eiffel Tower. This semantic resource is now lost. The usage has become addictive, so that we now read of, for example, King's College's chapel, instead of King's College Chapel. (A notably mindless example from *The Guardian*: "The US government argues that the rock's journey back to America was illegal."* This implies that the rock in question was endowed with volition. A counter example, where the genitive case is applied—to a proper noun, indeed, but to the wrong one—appears in *The Last Neanderthal*, by Ian Tattersall, Curator and Chairman of the Department of Anthropology at the American Museum of Natural History: "The darker side of Neanderthal nature . . . as exemplified by Gorganovic's alleged cannibalism."† Is Gorganovic, the academic, then, allegedly, a cannibal?)

I first noticed this consciously manipulated use of the genitive case in *Time* magazine—that very self-congratulating journal—in the mid-'50s; and now all journalists, and even those who should know better, have adopted this grammatical tic. An example of the deliberate and therefore meaningful use of the genitive applied to a collective noun occurs in E. Nesbit's *The Railway Children*:

> The platform round the door of the station had a dark blot round it, and the dark blot was a crowd of people. ... [The children] ran down the platform. When they got to the crowd, they could, of course, see nothing but the damp backs and elbows of the people on the crowd's outside.‡

Here, giving *crowd* the genitive case creates the impression of a single animate object—the sort of humorous touch altogether familiar in writing, and speaking, of that era. But who would grasp this fine

* 01.07.02   † p. 35
‡ 1990 Fabri Publishing facsimile reprint of 1906 edition, pp. 57–8

stroke, now? (*N.B.* The repetition of "dark blot", "platform" and "crowd" is a deliberate element of the creation of a sense of anticipation and focussing. This contrasts with the naïve type of repetition I refer to, below, when discussing *style*.)

A further curiosity about American English is that, whilst it is quite happy to produce a genitive case for any category of noun (see above), it actually fails to do so exactly where the sense seems most to require it: *barber shop* (in British English: *the barber's*), *hiker boots, designer clothes, farmer boy, boxer shorts, butcher knife, spider web, visitor center*. I used to think that *boxer shorts*—and, indeed, a *camper van*—were something quite different to what I later found them to be: underpants and a camping van. It was some time before I found out what was meant by *designer clothes*, namely, clothes made by a designer, *i.e.* designer's clothes. I have also seen, in a local shop, *Hiker Boots* (*i.e.* walking boots) and we now have, here, but presumably nationwide (*i.e.* nationally), *The Plumb Center*, and *The Builder Center*. (We had, already, in Sheffield a firm called *The Builders Centre*.)

I come now to a rather difficult area, already touched on above, relating to the nominal system: its patterning of determiners, and in particular the so-called definite, indefinite and "zero" articles. There is a disruption taking place, here, not perhaps quite equal in destructiveness to that occurring in the modal and tense systems but, taken in conjunction with the other disturbances to the nominal system I have described, serious enough.

First, it is necessary to say that, in "traditional" education, one of the shibboleths drummed into children was the distinction between *less* and *fewer*—

"More Haste, less Speed" *v.* "More Care, fewer Mistakes". Unfortunately, as was so often the case with traditional education, the matter was left, there, as a solitary stumbling block for the illiterate, rather than being related to the generalising categories of countable and uncountable nouns. I am not sure it was even extended to the counterparts *much* and *many.* (What is one to make of the phrases "much thanks" and "small thanks"?) Again, the application of *among[st]* and *amid[st]* is governed by the count/non-count noun categories: "He fell *amongst* thieves" as against "He was lost *amidst* the confusion". The Americans, again, can make nothing of this and even apply *among* where there are no more than two parties, that is where the dual, *between*, would be expected in British English.

An example of the extension of this confusion, from *Behind the Wall*, by Colin Thubron, an otherwise sensitive author: "Under the thatched eaves, *among* the smoke, the swallows are twittering in pairs."*

The nouns, as I have suggested, fall not only into the "traditional" categories of proper, abstract and concrete (which are semantic) but are (were) represented in the grammar itself both by their varying ability to attract determiners and intensifiers and in their ability to pluralise. To take a fairly easy example: on the A1 are to be seen notices reading "VISIT HISTORIC PETERBOROUGH" [*N.B.* zero determiner]. In terms of traditional British English, this notice implies that, somewhere, there must be another Peterborough, one which is, presumably, non-historic. Alternatively, *historic* can be construed as the epithet of *Peterborough* similar to, say, *Old*

* Page 269 of Penguin edition

Sarum, Great Missenden and *Long Melton*. However, we know now, though we didn't before, that the notice is shorthand for "VISIT THE HISTORIC TOWN OF PETERBOROUGH". It is the concrete noun *town* which can be qualified as historic, not the proper noun *Peterborough*. And, again, this practice of shorthand has been copied from the USA—and it entails a loss of meaning.

The application of the genitive case to this category of proper noun has already been remarked upon (*e.g.* London's Trafalgar Square) and what has happened, here, is that there is a confounding of the semantic categories of *personal* and *non-personal* proper noun. Similarly, it is now common to see such book titles as *Europe's Wild Flowers, The World's Oceans, Britain's Birds*, which would formerly (pre-1975) have been impossible. Compare these titles with *The Lays of Ancient Rome* (Ancient Rome's Lays), *The Last Days of Olwen* (Olwen's Last Days) or John James Audubon's *The Birds of America* (America's Birds).

The confounding of epithet with adjective (as in *Historic Peterborough*) and of epithet with noun-in-apposition appears again and again in the media—including the BBC. I first met this as a child in a picture book entitled *The Little History of the United States*, by Mabel Pyne (n.d. but bought for me in about 1943). In this (the pages are unnumbered) occurs the sentence:

> Angry Peter Stuyvesant, the Governor [of New Amsterdam] took down the Dutch flag, put up the English one and the name of the town was changed to New York.

As a child of seven, I thought *angry* was one of Peter

Stuyvesant's names. (I mean this quite genuinely; I am not faking.) British English would have had: "The angry Governor, Peter Stuyvesant . . ."

Perhaps the easiest way to look at this matter of category-collapse is by considering the incidence of *the*. This difficult word has, traditionally, been called "the definite article" and contrasted with the "indefinite article" *a / an*. However, unlike the latter, its semantic/conceptual range extends beyond what is implied by the terms "definite" and "indefinite". Its use and meaning is related to the other particles with initial /ð/: *this, these, that* (demonstrative adjective and pronoun), *that* (relative pronoun with variable vowel), *those, there* (demonstrative adverb), *there* ("dummy" pronoun /ðə/ as in "*there* was once a . . ." and which is phonologically indistinguishable, in pre-consonant position, from *the*), *thence, thither, then, than*. That is, the so-called definite article is part of the deixic potential of the language. (And this is not the same as what the philosophers call "the ostensive".) The "pointing" or "indicating" may be, indeed, at a concrete object *e.g.* "*the* car I am looking at", but it may be to a purely conceptual or generalising "object" *e.g.* "*the* car is a useful invention". It may, also, be a "pointing" to something mentioned previously or about to be mentioned; that is, it can be used anaphorically and cataphorically just as can the so-called demonstrative pronouns (*this, these, that, those*) *e.g.* "More people now drive but the number killed on the roads has declined" where the first *the* is anaphoric, referring back to *people*. (Compare: "More people now drive but those killed on the roads have declined in number" where the anaphora is supplied by *those* and where *number* has lost the "definite article"—because *the*, here, is NOT the definite article at all, that is, not the antithesis of *a*. It would take a foreigner to say: "More people now drive but those killed on the roads have declined in *the* number.")

I say "a foreigner", yet what are we, then, to make of such formulations as: "Numbers of people killed on the roads have declined", a construction now not-uncommon? Here is a confusion of the count/non-count categories and, in addition, catachresis in the entire semantic construction. It is a conflation, one supposes, of "The number of people killed . . . *has* declined" and "The numbers killed . . . *have* declined" where *numbers* is a pro-phrasal-noun for "the number of people".

This is a complex semantic/conceptual area of the language and one that occasions great difficulty to the Japanese, for instance, and yet one which is (was) essential—and taken for granted—in any moderately literate prose or poetry:

> . . . the big bare room . . . called Mother's work-shop. It had hardly any furniture. Just a table and a chair and a rug. But always big pots of flowers on the window-sills and on the mantelpiece. . . . And from the three long uncurtained windows the beautiful stretch of meadow and moorland, the far violet of the hills, and the unchanging changefulness of cloud and sky.*

A foreigner is likely to ask, "Why *the* beautiful stretch, *the* far violet and *the* unchanging changefulness? Aren't *stretch*, *violet* and *changefulness* qualities that cannot be pointed to by *the*? Why not *the* meadow and *the* moorland, *the* cloud and *the* sky—aren't these concrete nouns that, on the other hand, expressly require the article—they are not abstractions or general properties?"

* *The Railway Children, ed. cit.,* p. 114

But this taken-for-granted tact of the half-decent writer and speaker is now breaking down. Again, it is most apparent in American English, where we find *e.g.* "in light of these facts". The force of the structure *... the ... of ...* (*e.g.* "In *the* light *of* what is now known, *the* number *of* people killed is not surprising") is not recognised in A.E. Here, again, *the* is not the definite article; that is, it is not the counterpart of *a / an*. Note that *light* with zero determiner is equivalent to what is found in "VISIT [*the*] HISTORIC [*town of*] PETERBOROUGH".

Below is an example of the new "tactless" handling—*i.e.* conception—of abstract nouns (which, in this case, are converted adjectives):

> Many of Traherne's sources are exactly what one might expect from a well-educated man of his day—Plato and Aristotle, Augustine and Aquinas, the Bible, that blend of *[.]* classical and *[.]* religious that marked a traditional seventeenth-century education.*

Again, what is one to make of this sentence, representing a construction altogether common now in the press: "John Pilger's film about East Timor attracted three million viewers, of whom an extraordinary half a million called the switchboard afterwards."†

Is not this, also, foreigners' English? Well, yes, inasmuch as it originated in the USA (where it would be "a half million" rather than "half a million"). But what was extraordinary was, presumably, the *number* not the half-a-million—how can one abstract concept like half-a-million be any more extraordinary than another? Or did Mr Monbiot mean that it was those

---

* Denise Inge, *Thomas Traherne: Poetry and Prose*, 2002, p. xx.
† George Monbiot in *The Guardian*, 22.10.02, p. 19

viewers who "called the switchboard" who were extraordinary? If "half a million" is elliptical for "half a million viewers" (which, of course, it is) then how can the plural *viewers* attract the singular article *a / an*? Traditional English would have: "John Pilger's film about East Timor attracted three million viewers, half-a-million of whom rang the switchboard afterwards—an extraordinary number." Or ". . . an extraordinary number of whom, half-a-million, rang the switch-board" where "half-a-million" is in apposition with "a number".

These dislocations of grammar and semantics are driven by the journalistic mania for brevity and concision, which is thought to be achieved by the cutting-out of supposedly redundant words. But, I suggest, they could only have taken place, initially, in the USA because there so many have learnt Standard English as a second language/dialect and have, in consequence, never mastered its full intricacies. This, of course, is a politically out-of-bounds comment; those who control the media—journalists, T.V. and Radio presenters and their employers—are *ipso facto* correct—and let no dog bark!

The Americans are great ones for reducing derivatives to their base forms—and we, of course, tamely copy them after a short lapse of time:

> a *mix* = mixture (one now has a *mix* of people, ideas, *etc.* and also cake, trifle mix, *etc.* The word used to be applied to mortar and concrete.)
> *self-serve* = self-service
> *self-drive* = self-driving (*e.g.* van hire)
> a *pack* (*of*) = a packet, box, carton / a clutch (of), a bag (of). (Even a Marmite *jar* is now termed a *pack* on the label.)

easy cook = easy to cook / easily cooked
cookbook = cookery book (*cookbook* belongs also
    with *barbershop*—see above on genitives)
cookstove = cooking stove
frypan = frying pan (now beginning to appear in
    our shops)
start / finish line = starting / finishing line
race car = racing car
sailboat = sailing boat / ship
spark plug =sparking plug
swingarm = swinging arm (part of a motor-bike)
quick dry = quick-drying (*e.g.* paint)
yacht varnish = yachting varnish
shave cream = shaving cream
sort code = sorting code
surrounds = surroundings ("Madame de
    Pompadour portrayed . . . in more humble
    surrounds to appease her public."*)
scaffold = scaffolding (builders now mount a
    scaffold, like traitors).
timeshare = time-sharing (*cf.* ploughshare)
an upgrade = an upgrading
top-up = topping-up (*e.g.* phone card)
swimsuit = swimming costume (*suit* implies a set; a
    one-piece *swimsuit* is a contradiction in terms).
long-play record = long-playing record
the lead player = the leading player
gift-wrap = wrapping paper
spell-check = spelling-checker (this is ironic, given
    the context).
a frame-fit pump = a frame-fitting pump†
a think tank = a thinking tank (*i.e.* a tank for
    thinking in)
sex appeal / pervert / etc. = sexual appeal / pervert / *etc.*
climate change = climatic change
fashion [garments] = fashionable [garments]

I believe that these examples illustrate a collapse of
understanding of the meaning of the gerundial *-ing*

<hr>

* *The Guardian*, 10.10.02, p. 16   † heard in cycle shop on 18.07.02

form. (I take the *swimming* in "swimming costume" as a gerundial as it constitutes part of a phrasal noun.) This collapse also shows up in the phonology in terms of displaced stress: *shaving cream* is quite likely to have primary stress on *cream* instead of *shav(e)* without any recognition of distinction of meaning. Again, the distinction between, say, "a *sailing* boat" and "a sailing *boat*" used to be perfectly obvious to the speaker of B.E.

One of the effects of this practice is to produce a rhythm that is more staccato and thumping (but a lengthy note might be introduced here to do with the British pronunciation of *hostile, missile, civilisation, etc.* and the rhythmic implications of this, not least in poetry, since its evolution in the 19th century). The same effect is apparent from the, formerly typically American, pronunciations of `va `cate, `va `cation, `fa `tality, `pri `marily, `pa `rental, `pul `monary, `fre `quent (verb), `mo `ment, `ac `cent (both noun and verb), `non `sense, `fi `nance, `di `rect, `de `fect, `de `cipher, `de `moralise, `ro `mance, `ro `bust, `re `search, `re `source(s), `re `lapse, `re `cess and even, as I have heard, `re `sort, where both the first and second vowels are given major stress. We also find that there is a loss of distinction between the two former verbs orthographically represented by *replace*, which meant "to put back in its place" /`ri:pleɪs/ or "to substitute with something else" /rɪ`pleɪs/; similarly *redress*, which meant, according to stress-distribution, "to dress again" /`ri:drɛs/ or "to set right [an injury]" /rɪ`drɛs/. *Madman* is given equal stress on the two syllables so that there is no longer a semantic distinction between "*mad*man" and "mad *man*"; the same applies to *strawberry*, which I have heard even an English person pronounce as `straw `berry, that is, with two primary stresses together, and which phenomenon would, in

British English, be represented by an orthographic space between the stressed syllables. Again, American English makes no essential phonic distinction between the verbal and nominal forms of *ornament, accent, supplement, compliment, etc.* and this is likely to happen, here, shortly.

I think the first introductions of these typically American stress-forms were: `*finance,* `*direct,* `*digest* and `*defect.* They appeared during World War II, when American and Canadian servicemen were stationed in these islands; I recollect my father noting their appearance in the speech of one of his sons who hob-nobbed with the men. After the war, *not at all,* where the three syllables were given equal stress and even the orthographic spaces were given phonic representation gained a sort of "U" status. This was soon followed by *nonsense,* an uncountable noun, being rendered as *a* `*non* `*sense,* another example of two primary stresses falling on successive syllables within what is notionally one word (*cf.* also: `*pri* `*mate,* `*pri* `*mar*ily, `*ro* `*mance,* `*re* `*search,* `*de* `*mo*ralise, *etc.*).

Again, following American Speech, the B.E. stress-tone pattern has been reversed, so that the first rather than the last syllable has primary stress, in: `*armchair,* `*ice-cream,* `*weekend,* `*polar bear,* `*teddy-bear,* `*television,* `*Amsterdam* and, sometimes, in: `*kangaroo,* `*cigarette,* `*magazine,* `*margarine,* `*marzipan,* `*Parmezan,* `*Holderness.* Here, in Sheffield, the shopping mall of Meadowhall has likewise had its stress reversed, under the influence of the railway station recorded announcer (in R.P.).

Stress—and intonation—reversal is also found in the phrase *bye-bye.* In B.E., primary stress is on the first syllable and the tone, covering both syllables, is HIGH–MID; in A.E., this is reversed and the second syllable receives, in addition, GLIDING tone. This type of high and gliding tone was, once, the most noticeable—and alien—feature of American phonology and used to be guyed by speakers of B.E. when heard in, for instance, films ("I just *lur*ve the way you English *spe*ak. It's *re*al *cu*te!"). The mockery has given way to imitation in earnest.

One also now hears French loan words pronounced with would-be French stress, an innovation originating in the USA: *bla 'sé, bro 'chure, bu 'reau, a 'zure* and even *ca 'fé* and *de 'bris* /dəbri:/ (which last bears little resemblance, of course, to the French invariant plural *débris* /debri/). These are examples of *hypercorrection*—of which more, below.

(I take up the matter of phonological change, in further detail, later on.)

Another aside: the Americans seem to be averse to the *-ing* form in general, whether as gerund (*i.e.* noun) gerundive (*i.e.* adjective) or even present participle:

> *fasteners* = fastenings
> *fitments* = fittings
> *rental* = renting ("truck rental" in B.E. would be lorry renting"; in B.E. *rental* = income from rent).
> *a billboard* = a hoarding
> *a rendition* = a rendering
> *chicken wire* = wire-netting (in B.E. *chicken* is the young of the species).
> *climber rose* = climbing rose
> *pain reliever tablets* = pain relieving tablets
> *hiker boots* = walking boots
> *a part* = a parting (*e.g.* in the hair—not yet adopted here)
> *a cut* = a cutting (*i.e.* a road/railway cutting; in B.E. *a cut* = a canal).
> *a rocker* = a rocking chair (in B.E. the *rockers* = the feet of the chair).

a cooker = a (cooking) stove
the dishes = the washing-up (in B.E. *dishes* = large
  serving plates or a special preparation).
a bathrobe = a dressing gown
a vanity table = a dressing table
covers = bedding
the lounge = the sitting room
diner (car) = dining car (a *diner* in B.E. = one who
  dines)
a feel = a feeling/atmosphere (*e.g.* a Victorian
  feeling, a rustic feeling; in B.E. *a ... feel* = sensory
  touch, *e.g.* a rough feel)
the launch of = the launching of
design and build = designing and building (This is
  the new builders' slogan—*design* is, presumably, a
  noun; what, then, is *build*? A member of my
  family takes *Protein Build Powder*.)
"They were head*ed* west" (who headed them?)
"The hotel is nestl*ed* in the mountains" (who
  nestled it?)*

(If the *dumper truck, fork lift truck* and *camper van* had
been first developed in Britain, they would probably
have appeared as: *dumping wag(g)on, fork lifter* or
lifting trolley and *camping van*.)

An—educated—American once said to me, of his
bicycle: "The gears need adjusted." Again, American
English has: "He likes/loves to swim" (B.E. "He likes/
loves swimming"); "I wouldn't have you do that"
(B.E. "I wouldn't have you doing that". There is a
contrast in B.E. between *have X* + uninflected
infinitive (*i.e.* without *to*) and *have X* + present
participle.)

Again, American English follows CLAUSE + *rather
than* with the uninflected infinitive as against British
English CLAUSE + *rather than* followed by the present
participle (*e.g.* "She wants to see the world rather than

---

* See also the list above, which gives further examples.

stay home" *versus* "She wants to see the world rather than staying at home.") A typical example, frequently heard now in this country, would be: "My friend got a job rather than go to college."

This aversion may be what lies behind the abandoning of the present participle in captions, not only in newspapers but even in books and on the titles of CDs in favour of the present indicative, regardless of time period (*e.g.* "The Pope arrives yesterday"—a glorious absurdity*). Similarly, new developments are now billed as "Opens This Summer", *etc.* Note how a caption such as: "Wilhelm Kempf Playing the Beethoven Sonatas" is now cast as: "Wilhelm Kempf Plays Beethoven".

In the verbal system, we are seeing a gradual erosion (the computer tells me that this phrase is ungrammatical) of the distinction between the transitive and intransitive. The following verbs are, traditionally, transitive—they require an object:

> to relax (probably the first to arrive in Britain, the phrase "Oh, relax!" caused bewilderment at first.)
> to warn
> to cool
> to quit (of which the past tense, in British English, is *quitted* not *quit. Cf. knitted* and *wetted.*)
> to study
> to reduce
> to lower
> to level
> to fold
> to propagate
> to present
> to advise ("The Community Fund's lawyers have *advised* that there are no legal grounds . . ."†)
> to build

* *The Daily Telegraph*, 17.08.02, p. 15
† Gaby Hinsliff in *The Observer*, 13.10.02, p. 1

to seal
to ameliorate
to inflate
to stabilise
to erode (". . . even that rump territory was *eroding*
before Mr Arafat's eyes after . . . Israeli tanks
moved in . . . ."*)
to deplete ("Meanwhile . . . aquifers *deplete* and
cities demand ever more water."†)
to enjoy
to obsess
to foment (presumably a confusion with *to ferment*:
"How often places of beauty are those where
wars *foment*."‡ *Cf.* confounding of *instigate* and
institute.)

Now, pensions *reduce,* the air pressure *lowers,*
politicians *warn* or *quit,* Mr Bush *obsesses* and we all
enjoy.

On the other hand, if these verbs are now
intransitive, then it should, traditionally, be impossible to apply the passive voice to them, because
they lack an object to take subject position—but this
is not so; the categories here, also, are breaking down.
(Note, also, the list of denuded phrasal verbs given
above where, even in their stripped form, they are
treated as intransitives, *e.g.* "The Metropolitan Borough
of South Yorkshire *folded* in 1987"; "Global temper-
atures are *warming*"; *etc.*)

Overall, however, there is a general reduction in
the use of the passive voice, whether in spoken or
written English. My son was, indeed, advised by his
tutor not to employ it in his PhD thesis. I think the
connexion between this and the use of converted
active verbs is clear: "Lobes of high pressure cold air

* *The Guardian,* 25.06.02
† *The Guardian,* 22.08.02, Earth Supplement, p. 37
‡ Giles Foden in *The Guardian,* 26.08.02, p. 13

force out over the Mid-West"; "The mountains start to erode"; *etc*. It cannot be a coincidence that the computer tool "Spelling and Grammar: English [United Kingdom]" questions the passive voice whenever it appears. (I refer to the malign linguistic influence of the computer, again, below.)

The loss of the passive voice with its attendant shift of focus in written English is paralleled by an equivalent loss in speech, where the tonic stress now tends to fall on the final element of the clause regardless of the intended meaning. Thus, one hears: "It's not my *fault*" with *phonic* stress on "fault" where the *conceptual* emphasis is on "my".

One might, now, be asked the question: "Is this your *car / house / dog / etc.*?" where the issue is not the car / house / dog / *etc*. but the possessor thereof. This confusion is allied with the obliteration of syntactically emphatic structures such as:

"Is this car/house/dog/*etc. yours*?"
"Is it *you* who own this car/house/dog/*etc*?"*

One supposes that these structures are now felt to lack street-cred.

Indeed, even trained actors now seem to have lost the sense of where to place this stress; in a current reading of the *Just William* stories, William is rendered as saying: "How was I to *know*?" where the context clearly indicates that he says: "How was *I* to know?"—a locution once all too familiar from a righteous child. Richmal Crompton took it for granted that her readers would recognise this, but even this level of writing is becoming, it would seem, too difficult for us.

This shifting of tonic stress to the end of the tone-group leads also to a failure to distinguish, in ripostes,

---

* See also the entries on page 22.

between *denial* and *contradiction / rejection.* Thus might occur the following exchange:

> *Parent*: You've been at the Christmas cake again!
> *Child*: No, I haven't! [*No, I haven't! contra* No, I haven't!]

The modern child produces only the latter.

Again, the distinction between the stressed and unstressed phonic forms of the personal pronouns is being lost on this side of the Atlantic as it has already been on the other. Thus, we now find an inability either to speak or to comprehend the differences between:

> He /hɪ/ gave it to me /mɪ/.
> He /hi:/ gave it to me /mɪ/.
> He /hɪ/ gave it to me /mi:/.

What has been lost, here, is very serious indeed and to attend a dramatic performance given by, say, students is to undergo an experience of linguistic and conceptual anguish.

The abandonment of the passive voice shows up in both newspapers and academic papers, where one encounters sentences which read like the decontextualised sentences formerly given at school for translation into a foreign language. An example from *The Times*: "Country seat: William Shenstone began the trend."* The topic is not, as the grammar implies, William Shenstone, but outdoor benches. What was meant is: "The trend was begun by William Shenstone." Another example, from *The Sunday Times*: "Alasdair Palmer argues that judges determine the asylum law."† What is the theme—"judges", "asylum law" or "determine"? Presumably, what was intended is: "Alasdair Palmer argues that it is judges

---

* 10.08.02, p. 3   † 02.06.02

who determine the asylum law" or: "Alasdair Palmer argues that the asylum law is determined by judges."

There is also a marked reduction in the incidence of non-finite clauses. An example of the extension of finite clause use is this: "Headmasters demand all papers must be re-marked" [*i.e.* "Headmasters demand the re-marking of all papers"].* Typically, one sees/ hears: ". . . to the extent that it was useless" [B.E. ". . . to the extent of being useless"]; "The government demanded that he be extradited" [B.E. "The government demanded his extradition"].

The American adverb and adverbial phrase now feature frequently on this side of the Atlantic. So much is this the case that the British English meaning is now lost in: *routinely* (= *thoughtlessly, inattentively,* NOT "as a matter of routine" [*cf.* French: *de routine* and *routinier*]), *hopefully* (= *wishfully, wishingly,* NOT "let us hope so"), *presently* (= *soon, shortly,* NOT "at the present" [*cf.* the confusion over *anon*]), *importantly* (= *portentously, bombastically,* NOT "this is a matter of great import"), *surely* (= *one hopes,* NOT "certainly"), and *famously* (= *famously,* NOT "notoriously"). We also find *that way* for: *in that way / like this / like that / so. To the extent that . . .* replaces: *inasmuch as / in so far as / in that / to such an extent that* + clause / *to the extent of* + *ing* phrase / *to the point where . . .* Again, *likely* is used in American English as an adverb: "It likely will happen" (B.E. "It is likely to happen"). Shall we soon be hearing "They friendly met" and "She ugly looked at him"?

A small point: even our politicians now use the American intensifier *overly* (*e.g.* "I am not overly concerned"). It is not any more intensive than plain *over* and probably derives from a confusion/con-

* *The Guardian,* 19.09.02, p. 1

flation with *unduly*. I have yet to hear *underly*, but one does hear and see—half-humorously—*muchly*, and I have heard a member of my family say *seldomly*. I have also read *contrarily* in one of Helen Rumbelow's articles in *The Times*. She meant *on the other hand* or *contrariwise*. But it is a telling fact that what she wrote was passed by the editor. (The computer questions the passive voice, here, to offer this improvement: "The editor passed a telling fact that what she wrote".)

An aspect of American adverbial syntax beginning to appear, and be heard, here is the placing of the adverb BEFORE the copula and BEFORE the auxiliary verb and the main verb; this is the unmarked norm in American English, whereas in B.E. it marks an emphasis; *e.g.* "It often is the case that . . ."; (in B.E., the verb, here, is emphatic implying a contradiction of the contrary suggestion *i.e.* "It's never the case that . . ."); "He probably will arrive after dinner"; (in B.E., "probably" in this position implies a correction of a misapprehension, *e.g.* "He will arrive . . . possibly"). Note, also, the phrase now frequently heard, here: "It certainly is" (*contra* "Certainly, it is").

I have not studied the records closely, but I suspect that there have been, and are still, some quite serious misunderstandings created by these differences in adverbial semantics and syntax. What would the Americans, the British, the Pakistanis and the Indians make of the sentence: "There *surely* will be war between these nations"? ("But [the bomb in Bali] does *surely* demonstrate that the threat . . . symbolised by al-Qaida remains undiminished."* Does this mean "definitely" or "wouldn't you agree"?)

Again, the phrase "It certainly *is*" is, in British English, not an affirmation, as in American, but a denial:

---

* *The Guardian*, 14.10.02, leading article

> Y: Surely, it's not going to snow, is it?
> Z: It certainly *is*!

A relatively small point: the movement towards analysis continues, with *one time* for *once*, *two times* for *twice*, *two weeks* for *fortnight*. Only the elderly are now heard to say the last. I think this is connected, also, with the loss of the collective nouns: *dozen*, *score*, *a chest* (of drawers), *a bunch* (of keys), *a flight* (of steps). I have heard all the last three collected under *a set*. (See also the remarks, above, concerning *sports*, viz. *sport* car, *sport* socks, *etc*. And underpants are now offered as *slip*, *brief* and *trunk*.)

Something not mentioned, explicitly, so far is prose style, as against the dialogue style discussed above. One of the most significant changes, here, is a breaking-down of linguistic textual cohesion. This shows itself in two chief ways: a great reduction in sub-ordination, especially of non-finite clauses ("phrases" in traditional grammar) and a tendency to repeat, sometimes even within the same sentence, the nouns, even the topic noun. A fairly typical example of the latter is this:

> Florence Hodgson has overseen the *library* for 55 years but nowadays there is no demand for the *library*. The *library* has been unused for the last three years.*

This reads almost like Dalek language, that is, citation sentences. Note, also here, the active voice in the first sentence where the topic is not the subject but the object of the verb.

Further examples, here from web-site information on knee-replacement operations:

---

* *The Daily Telegraph*, 21.06.01

> It is important that you understand that there
> are *risks* associated with . . . total knee replace-
> ment. . . . These *risks* include the *risk* of death.
> However, the *important* thing to understand is
> that it is motion without pain that is *important.*

My record in this respect is the occurrence of *egg* nine
times in eight lines in a circular from the Yorkshire
Geological Society. (They were dinosaur eggs, not
hen's.)

The defence of this phenomenon may be that it
ensures more perfect comprehension in the reader,
that it leaves no room for misunderstandings. If this is
so, then I would suggest that this implies a serious
decline in readers' powers of comprehension—that is,
in their ability to construe; and competence in
reading—and listening—are as much part of the
language as are writing and speaking.

Another loss to textual cohesion is the abandoning
of the *this* / *that* contrast where reference is made
back (anaphora). What was last spoken of was *this,*
what was earlier spoken of was *that.* One finds, now,
that *that* alone is used, *e.g.*

> These risks include the risk of death. *That*'s true
> of any major surgical procedure.[*]

> Variation in the amount of CO_2 in the atmosphere
> is usually taken to be the main cause of climate
> change. The apparent exceptions to the link
> threaten to undermine *that.*[†]

Note, also, the supersession of the pro-clause *so* by
that. "I wouldn't dare do *so*" becomes "I wouldn't dare
do *that*". The line in *Lavender's Blue* "Who told you
so?" will have to be rewritten as "Who told you that?"

[*] Web page on joint-replacements
[†] Lee R. Kump, *Nature*, 408, 2000, p. 651

Another aspect of style is the confusion of the registers of formality—something that used to be the hallmark of police constables and town-hall officials. (See also remarks, below, on the Liza Doolittle Syndrome.) The salutation of one addressing a learned society is now less likely to be "Ladies and Gentlemen . . ." than "O.K., so . . ." And the address will conclude not with ". . . and, finally, Ladies and Gentlemen . . ." but with ". . . and that's it!" Governments are no longer overthrown; they are *toppled*. Volcanoes invariably *spew* lava. Ships now *hit* rocks, muggers *hit* their victims and people are *hit* by lightning. Letters from banks and the *utilities* (*i.e.* public services) are written with the contracted forms formerly reserved for familiar correspondence and speech: *we're, we'll, you're, can't* (but, note, never *mayn't, mightn't* or *mustn't*—presumably because these, as I was once informed by a school-pupil, do not exist). My daughter-in-law, when applying for a school-teaching post, was saluted with *Hi* in the formal written acknowledgement from the head-teacher. On the back of Transco vans is written "Smell gas?"—a direct transcript from a style proper to spoken, not written, language and which, again, has been copied from the USA, where deletion of the subject pronoun and auxiliary verb in interrogatives became idiomatic—when, I do not know. The counterpart of this chumminess—or blarney—is that bills are now always the customer's not the provider's (*your bill* not *our bill* nor even *the bill*).

The Royal Family is now referred to as *the Royals* even in the so-called quality papers and by the attendant at Osborne House. Our politicians, without the least appearance of embarrassment in themselves or of mockery from the public, utter such phrases as *lone parents, garbagegate, dumbing down, New Deal, bullshit* and *zero tolerance* and our local police force is happy to label itself *Crimebusters*. Princess Diana, on the occasion of her wedding, was described by the BBC commentator in these words: "And, oh, she's absolutely *gift-wrapped*". Perhaps, it was scarcely surprising that this lady (who, according to her brother, was *raised*) later accused her mother-in-law of "*calling all the shots*". The phrases *for free, for real* and *king-size* were originally intended humorously but, now, who can tell whether the Royals are for real or for free or, indeed, whether they shouldn't be toppled as being too big for their king-size? Would it be possible for Mark Twain to find an audience that understood him, today?

Robin Cook, the erstwhile representative of this nation to foreign powers, said recently in the Commons, "It's important that it's Saddam Hussein and not *us that is* seen as in the wrong." So much for a sense of style and occasion—not to mention common-and-garden "grammar". ("It is important that it should not be we who are seen as in the wrong but Saddam Hussein.")

In the matter of the phonology of the language, the most serious change lies in the realm of intonation. English is (was) a tone language, but, unlike in Chinese, the tones are (were) applied to the phrase and clause. Indeed the major categories of modality (indicative, interrogative, imperative, emphatic, exclamatory) are (were) represented by the intonation—and it is (was) in fact possible to utter a single word in any one of the modal categories, making a one-word sentence (*e.g.* "yes", "no" , "you", "me", *etc.*). Listen to a group of students relaxing in the café or bar; is it possible to distinguish the modality of their sentences by their intonation? If every clause has a rising tone, then that tone loses its meaning, for tones, like phonemes, only work contrastively. Incidentally, the tone used is not what would traditionally have been the simple interrogative but is nearer to "question-response", that is the questioning of a preceding statement. However, the overall context contradicts this interpretation so that the tone no longer has any linguistic meaning— though it certainly has a cultural one, namely "I belong to the group that sounds like this."

Various other things are happening in the phonology—centralising of the vowels; *book, good, put, bull,* are now, even by the BBC, given the schwa vowel /ə/, which is the first time in history, I believe, that this has received the status of a stressed vowel. (It is also now heard in the second syllable of *because* /bɪkəz/.) *You, rude, news, choose, etc.* are moving near the French vowel [y] in *tu, cru, brut.* (See also remarks, below, on *inherent, etc.*)

We are witnessing in adult speech what has been hitherto one of the marks of immature speakers, consonant exchange, the most familiar of which were /k/ and /g/ for /t/ and /d/ ("There's a lickle pussy in the miggle of the pond"). The most notable, in present adult speech, is the replacement of intervocalic /t/ by the glottal stop [ʔ], and this is now appearing even in stage speech, at word-end especially ("puʔ iʔ on", "geʔ iʔ off", "noʔ aʔ all" OR "noʔ at all"). Once again, one looks for a cultural significance in this—who are they who are being thus imitated? Incidentally, one can detect the glottal stops in a speaker not one word of whose utterance can otherwise be interpreted on account of distance or interference.

The "reduced" –ing form conventionally written as *doin'*, *feelin'*, *etc.*, is, in fact, another example of consonant replacement: /ŋ/ is a velar whilst /n/ is an alveolar articulation. This, of course, has a long history (Pope rhymes *Helen* with *compelling* and Wordsworth *sullen* with *culling*), but it is rapidly becoming universal, now including even "good" speakers and formal situations.

What else? Where there is (was) a distinction marked by stress between the nominal and verbal form of the same "word", the nominal form is now applied uniquely. I have heard all the following pronounced with stress on the first syllable where the syntax marked the item as a verb:

> *pro*test
> *pro*gress
> *pro*spect
> *sus*pect
> *sur*vey [first heard from an archaeologist—I
>   thought, initially, that he meant it as a verbal
>   distinction from sur*vey*.]
> *dis*charge
> *per*vert
> *fre*quent
> *in*crease
> *trans*fer
> *trans*port

and, quite incredibly, one might think: *en*velope

This last appeared in an ITV programme about flooding in Mozambique where, the presenter informed us, groups of people were about to be *en*veloped by flood-waters. The impression was worthy of Groucho Marx—but not a grimace from anyone else of the group of students and their lecturer (a geographer). (*Par contre*, several times, I have heard *estimate* in its nominal form used for the verb—for example from this same geographer. Confusion reigns, and there is some connection, here, with *spelling pronunciation*, of which I say more, below.)

The stressing of *contribute* and *distribute* on the first syllable also falls into this new, simplified, pattern (compare *attribute* in its verbal and nominal phonic forms). One would expect *alternate* soon to undergo a similar effect. (American English seems to lack the form *alternative*.)

The "e" vowel in the following has been (is being) "weakened" (centralised), again under the same influence: *inherent* (but not in: *coherent, adherent*), *genus, fetid, ephemeral, centenary, economic, evolution, emanate* (this has led one manufacturer to write "emernate" on his packaging (*i.e.* wrapping)). This is a type of spelling pronunciation, but based on mistaken notions about the relationship between sound and orthography—as is the case with the displacing of stress to the second syllable of: *harass, goddess, princess;* but, in point of fact, there are two misconceptions at work, here, which are in conflict with each other and which lead to a further muddling of the phonology-orthography relationship. (A doubled consonant does NOT necessarily mark a stressed syllable *e.g. necessarily, dissolve, desiccate, tariff, sheriff, succumb, suggest, allot, idyll, parallel, satellite, Purcell, Lyell, Marvell* (*cf. marvellous*); and note these couplets: co`rral/`coral, de`ssert/`desert, `canvass/`canvas, `label/la`pel [NOT lapell], `anal/ca`nal [NOT canall], `rebel *n.*/re`bel *vb.* [NOT rebbel AND rebell], *etc.*)

Aside: Teachers have been, and still are, quite incapable of either seeing or teaching the systemic patterning of English spelling. And this is not at all a trivial matter, for language, in a literate society, does exist in two modes, spoken and written, and the interaction between them is very complex. One of the unfortunate effects of orthographic form is to make us imagine a silence equivalent to the space between written words. This can lead, in reading, to a hiatus which interrupts the continuity of the speech sound. It is not uncommon to hear this on the BBC and from professional actors, especially where the "gap" is bounded by vowels (*e.g.* "He s*aw* . . . *i*t in m*y* . . . *ey*es.") This is also the case where the word preceding the "gap" ends in "r" and where, traditionally, the "r" was sounded (*e.g.* "I saw it in the*ir* eyes"). This latter hiatus is, presumably, due to the fear of obtruding an "intrusive *r*" (*e.g.* "I saw *r*it in their eyes").

There is a strong case for spelling reform but this would not be a light undertaking, and it would require a book to itself!

A perhaps not-so-minor agent of linguistic change is what, I suppose, one might call the Liza Doolittle Syndrome [LDS]—the rise to positions of power and authority by lower-class people who have never altered their "grammar" (*i.e.* the school-teacher's notion of grammar). This has meant that the double auxiliary in, for instance, "It didn't use*d* [*sic*] to be" (seen in *The Guardian*—I, myself, have been; "corrected"—by a foreigner—for saying "He usedn't to do it") and even "It didn't ought to be" have become Standard. One regularly hears: "If he'd've done it . . ." and, grandiloquently, "Had he've done it". I have seen, in essays: "If X had have happened . . ." (uncorrected by the tutor). Other examples include: "You couldn't hardly see it / you couldn't see it, hardly" ("Nexia's farm manager tells me 'We can't hardly control them'."*); failure of distinction between

* *The Sunday Telegraph*, magazine', 21.07.02, p. 27

some and *any*, on the one hand, and between *either* and *as well*, on the other, in relation to the positive and the negative (*e.g.* "I couldn't find something", "He isn't coming, as well"). The reduction of the question-response *Why?* and *Why not?* to *Why?* with rising gliding intonation is also an example of the loss of distinction between the positive and negative semantic (see, above, comparative table of "new" and B.E.).

The reduplicated subject is now also very common in speech: "The manager (yeah) he said . . . / The politicians (yeah) they want . . . / My Dad (yeah) he thinks . . ." Not only Liza Doolittle but Huck Finn went in for this—sans "yeah", of course—and so do modern Oxbridge students. And here is an example from *The Guardian*:

> "Reefs, if they are left alone and not stressed, they will recover quite rapidly," said Dr Clive Wilkinson, who heads the Global Reef Monitoring Network.*

Whether it was Dr Wilkinson or the *Guardian* reporter who perpetrated this we have, given the laxness of media probity, no way of telling.

It is interesting to note the absence from the speech of younger people of any social class of (a) the reduplicated comparative (*e.g. more uglier*) and (b) the reduplicated negative (*e.g. You don't know nothing*); again, "dropped aitches" and the weak form of *my* and *one* /mɪ/ /ən/ are becoming rarities. I think that this is due to the fact that, traditionally, these have been denounced as Bad English by teachers and high-lighted by second-rate novelists and dramatists in their representation of lower-class speech. The fact that the educated and upper classes also perpetrated these supposed enormities in given syntactic and

---

* 18.12.02, p. 13

social contexts has gone quite unobserved—except by poets and phoneticians (Hopkins rhymed *communion* with *boon he on**).

Another indicator of, what formerly would have been classed as, uneducated speech is: "There was this man, right, he . . ." where *this* is exophoric, that is, non-textual. Basil Bernstein, back in the '70s, gave this as an example of what he called "Restricted Code", the code of socially implicit and taken-for-granted meanings that characterised, and educationally restricted, his group of London messenger boys. Somewhat akin to this example is the use of *them* as a generic intensive/emphatic pronoun, whereas educated speech required a distinction between *them* (inanimate) and *those* (animate)—hence the alteration in the Lord's Prayer of "we forgive them that trespass" to "we forgive those who trespass". And, of course, this leads back to what is described above concerning the distinctions between *who*, *which* and *that*.

Yet another element of the LDS which has become "accepted" is the inability to distinguish between the gerund and the present participle in such a construction as: "Him turning up late made me miss my train." One now finds even RP-speaking MPs failing to make the distinction.

A good example of what this leads to is supplied by *The Guardian*:

> Trust gardens are planned in advance and already different species are being planted to avoid [*sic*] them dying in what would be a hostile climate in 30 years. [What, in any case, does *them* refer to?]†

As with several other examples quoted from the

---

* "The Bugler's First Communion", lines 5 & 8

† 20.11.02, p. 3

"quality" newspapers, one longs to believe that the writer had his linguistic tongue in his cheek.

The LDS has also led to the enshrining of hyper-corrections such as "between you and he", "to my husband and I" and spelling pronunciations (pro*nou*nciations [*sic*] according to the prospectus of Sheffield University English Language Department) such as *almond* /ælmənd/, *sandwich* /sændwɪtʃ/, *forehead* /fɔːhɛd/, *respite* /rɛspaɪt/, *ate* /eɪt/, *exit* /ɛksɪt/, *spelled* /spɛld/, *spilled* /spɪld/, *Uttoxeter* /juːtɒksɪtə/ *etc*.

The geography lecturer already alluded to also says *Campbell* /kampbɛl/ and *width* /wɪdð/, the latter of which I have never heard from anyone else.

What is not generally remarked is that spelling pronunciations issue from a naïve literalism, a form of pedantry, in fact. It is curious how angry or suspicious many people become when faced with *Cholmondeley* /tʃʌmlɪ/, *Mainwaring* /mænərɪŋ/, *Scone* / skuːn/, *Glamis* /glɑːmz/, *Crich* /kraɪtʃ/, *Alnwick* /anɪk/, *McGrath* /məgraː/, *Strachan* /strɔːn/, *etc*., denouncing this as affectation whilst seeing none in the received pronunciations of *Gloucester, Leicester, Worcester, Folkestone, Salisbury, Durham, Southwark, Woolwich, London, Thames, England, etc*. The, largely unconscious, view is that these latter "say" the received pro-nunciations, whilst the former do not. (There is some psycho-linguistic puzzle to work out, here, as I have taught enough foreign students to know that the phenomenon is not confined to native English speakers. I failed to persuade a visiting Japanese lecturer of the received pronunciations of *Oxford, Chatsworth* and *Warwick*.)

I think there is something at work, an unreflecting attachment to the letter-sounds inculcated in the

Infants School, when even anthropologists pronounce *primate* as /praɪmeɪt/ rather than /praɪmɪt/. There is a failure to see the word as based on *prime* and not on *mate*; and this is similar, indeed, to the tacit belief that *covert* is simply *overt* with a "c" in front and that *respite* has some connection with *spite*. (Teachers of reading encourage their pupils to look for "words" they know within words they do not. Thus *thinking* might be interpreted as *thin king*, and *carpet* as *car pet*. The English have, in consequence, got not no clue but the wrong clues to giving a phonological representation of written words of more than one syllable and a graphological representation of any newly-encountered spoken words.)

The following are, perhaps, not quite spelling pronunciations but examples of unawareness of the appropriate paradigm and the application of a less sophisticated, or more "primitive", one:

congratu`latory
partici`patory
cele`bratory
compen`satory
man`datory
mi`gratory
vege`tative
quanti`tative
quali`tative
medi`tative
contem`plative

These are of the same sort as ad*mir*able, com*par*able, and la*ment*able. Overall, there is a marked reduction in the incidence of the rhythm typified by *aristocrat*. I have heard a*mic*able and, even from university lecturers, prac*tic*able, inera*dic*able, inex*or*able.

The LDS has also been a major force for poshification in the adoption of American genteelisms or hypertrophisms: *bathroom, restroom* (my comprehensive-educated son tells me that "lavatory" is a horrid word), *apartment* (what does the new man make of the phrase "private apartments"?), home ("house", "dwelling", "place"), *mobile home* ("caravan"), *master bedroom* ("main bedroom"), *location* ("situation", "position", "site", "setting", "spot"), *executive* ("manager"), *to commute* ("to travel in/up (to town)") *engineer* ("mechanic"/"repair man"), *senior citizen* ("OAP"), *elderly people* ("old folk"), *rest home* ("old folks' home"), *student* ("pupil"/"scholar"), *auto* ("car"), *used* ("second-hand"—even clothes are now *used* rather than "worn"), *rooster* ("cock"/"cockerel"—this pitiful American euphemism has appeared even in *The Times*), *hospitalized* ("in hospital"—but, note, *institutionalized* does NOT mean "in an institution"). A further, now common, hypercorrection of American origin is: "How *may* I help you?"

Why American? I think because this is seen as bypassing the social-class system of this country and rendering it irrelevant. Incidentally, I think this phenomenon has also accelerated the decline of the modal system and, with it, the modally constructed subjunctive and the subjunctive forms of *to be* ("If I were you . . ." and "as it were" cause nervousness in the newly-educated). Contrariwise, the non-modal subjunctive, as practised in the USA, is readily accepted here: "It's a good idea that he be informed"; "The judge ordered that the defendant be acquitted"; "The P.M. demanded that he speak." Note, also, the appearance here, now, of "Be aware that . . ."; "Be sure to take your belongings" (B.E. "Make sure you take . . .") *"Be sure your sins will find you out"* must occasion more brain-teasing than heart-searching, nowadays.

A further type of genteelism is seen in the application of a pseudo-Latin plural to words ending in *-us*, regardless of whether they derive from that language or not, and more particularly when they are felt to be a little exotic. Thus we see—and hear of— not only *cacti, fungi, gladioli, croci* but also *hippopotami* and *octopi* (which last appeared in *Quaternary News*, the journal of the Quaternary Research Association. My computer questions *octopi* but not *hippopotami*!) The Americans say, with straight faces, *syllabi*. The most egregious example I have seen of this type of hyper-correction appears in a public notice in Sherwood Forest drawing our attention to its "mushrooms and fungi's".

The acceptance of the replacement of inter-vocalic /t/ by the glottal stop /ʔ/ is also an element of the LDS, as is that of *like* used as a subordinator, both of which phenomena I have discussed above in another context.

Another, and very minor, former LDS indicator is the failure to distinguish between *all*, *all of* and *the whole of.* The saying "You can fool some of the people some of the time but you can't fool all of the people all of the time" was recognised as, at least, non-Standard. An educated person would not have said, as I have recently heard a senior university lecturer say, "all of France". (This same lecturer also consistently treated *phenomena* and *criteria* as singulars and pronounced *debris* /dəbriː/.) I say "very minor", yet there are instances where it is less so, as in the following (from a water board insurance scheme):

> Remember, membership gives you all of these benefits.

The intended meaning, judging from the context, is

"all these [*i.e.* those listed] benefits"; not "all of" as opposed to "some of ". I give, here, an example of the fully literate use of *all of* . . .

> Papal politics and cupidity seemed to [Dante] to be what had plunged all of Italy into strife, and much of Europe too.*

Here, Maurice Keen is making an emphatic parallel between Italy and Europe.

The otiose *of* in phrases such as "Get off of it!" "Get outside of it!", which were regarded as almost stage Cockney, now actually appear in supposedly educated English: "The tools . . . were rather crude, consisting of small pebbles with flakes bashed off of them."†

A more serious LDS indicator was the confusion of *to lie* (*down*) and *to lay* (*down*), that is, between the intransitive and the transitive verbs. This led, for example, to the hyper-correct "Just lie the books here." But, note, this was not a U/non-U distinction any more than was "to my husband and I/me", except that the U may have imagined that it was only the non-U who got these things wrong! I have seen *lay* used intransitively in *The Times*—though, to be fair, this was in quoting an American. The following quotation, however, is from James Meek, the science correspondent of *The Guardian*:

> Scientists have long predicted that black holes lay at the centre of galaxies.‡

Or is this an example of confusion of tenses? One simply cannot tell. And again, what is the topic— black holes or galaxies? The suspicion that Mr Meek is using *lay* intransitively (confusing it with *lie*) is

---

* Maurice Keen, *The Pelican History of Medieval Europe*, 1969, p. 219
† Ian Tattersall, *The Last Neanderthal*, p. 54
‡ 17.10.02, p. 15

reinforced by his later usages: "*unmeasurably* vast" and "Our sun, and *us* with it, takes 230m years to orbit the galaxy." This is the grammar of the new man.

Yet another, former, LDS indicator was the use of the same form for both the simple past and the past participle in, notoriously, the verbs *do* and *go* [done, gone], less notoriously in *begin, swim, sing, ring, spring, hang* and, least so, in *thrive* and *hang*. Yet, now, one finds *swum, sung, rung* and *sprung* appearing as the simple past tense of their respective verbs; I have seen *swum* in *The Times* and this sentence, by a senior research fellow at the LSE, appears in *The Guardian*: "The European convention sprung from the UN's Universal Declaration of Human Rights."*

That, in Jane Austen and her predecessors, the convention in this respect was the reverse does not negate the fact that a distinction was made between past participle and preterite; the point is that this is now lost.

Again, Liza Doolittle did not know the difference between *older* and *elder*—or, rather, was ignorant of the latter—and such is the case with *The Times*, too, now.

Another aspect of the LDS is inverted snobbery. It is this which has led to the rejection of the supposedly posh "*You and I* + verb" in favour of the supposedly demotic "*Me and you* + verb". I have heard a quite explicit linking of the former with The Queen, *etc.*

Furthermore, I suspect that the whole category of reflexive pronouns is in process of disappearing. It is now common to hear people say "I bought it for me", "She got it for her". The new, that is "cool", multiple-pronoun subject cases are "*Me and X / Us and them* are going out . . ." *etc.* This is, as I have said, a rejection of the supposedly posh "*X and I* are going out" . . . *etc.*

* 03.10.02, p. 20

but it is also suggestive that the pronouns chosen should be *me, us, them* rather than *myself, ourselves, themselves.* A quotation from *The Guardian* may help to show this process at work:

> Hewitt has become notorious for his attempts to sell the correspondence between him and Princess Diana, and is held in contempt by the tabloid press.*

The *him* reads as a reference to someone who is NOT Hewitt!

One consequence of the "acceptance" of the LDS is the disappearance of social class linguistic distinctions, at least in writing. When, for instance, Joanna Trollope attempts to distinguish her characters, socially, in the dialogue, she can only do so by invoking "old-fashioned" speech-forms which, consistently enough, she applies to the oldest generation. The middle and young generations are quite unplaced by their speech—unless it is by their swearing. This, no doubt, reflects the current social reality, but it makes for a curious anonymity and shapelessness in these characters. I wonder whether anyone below the age of, say, 50 would have the least glimmering of the linguistic ironies in Muriel Spark's *You Should Have Seen the Mess.*

I have suggested that a type of literalist pedantry is one of the elements of the LDS. But pedantry, of course, does not obtain merely here. There is another type, which conflates the grammatical and semantic systems and goes about to force the former to conform with the latter. Thus we find "immune *from*" and "forbidden *from*". It was interesting to see that oracle of right-thinking, Auberon Waugh, falling into this particular mire! But, then, even F. R. Leavis wrote "averse *from*". As a clear example of the lack of

---

* Matt Wells, media correspondent, 15.01.03, p. 2

one-to-one correspondence between the grammatical
and the semantic, consider the sentence:

> Were you thinking of paying, perhaps, for the
> damage you have caused?

Grammatically, this is interrogative, but semantically
(*i.e.* culturally) imperative. The required answer is not
"yes" or "no" but "If you insist" or "Of course; don't
think any further of it!"

When, one might ask, did these changes begin in
this country? I think the great turning point was *circa*
1975. I think it is possible to do an "unseen" of 20th-
century writing and to date it as either pre- or post-
that point; it is even possible to detect emendations
or additions made to pre-'75 works which themselves
post-date it. Here follows a short passage from a book,
Engineering in the Ancient World, by J. G. Landels, first
published in 1978, by Chatto and Windus, and
reprinted in 1997 by Constable & Co. To make good
my point about dating: the author consistently uses
around throughout the entire book. He also has *back
and forth* for *to and fro* (for which latter phrase the
computer "spell-check [English: United Kingdom]"
suggests *to and frog*).

> From about the middle of the eighth century B.C.
> there appear in vase-paintings ships with two
> superimposed banks of oars. This change was
> accompanied by another, which must have been
> known in Homer's time but is not mentioned by
> him—perhaps because he wished in this matter to
> maintain a "genuine antique touch". In order to
> make it possible for ships to carry a landing-party,
> or to fight at sea by drawing alongside and
> attacking each others' [*sic*] crews (Homer has no
> occasion to mention either of these operations), a

raised deck was built, running the whole length of the ship but not the whole width. A space of 3 ft or so was left undecked along either side to give headroom for the rowers and avoid the danger of their being trapped below deck at the mercy of a boarding-party.*

Here follows a *rendition* (*i.e.* rendering) into "modern" English. The only lexical alteration I make is of "m" for "ft"; neither do I change the order of the sentences.

Ships with two superimposed banks of oars appear in vase-paintings from about the middle of the 8th century b.c. This change accompanied another change about which Homer's time must have known but Homer does not mention this change maybe because he wished to maintain a "genuine antique touch". Ship builders built a raised deck running the ship's whole length but not the ship's whole width. This was in order to make it possible for ships to carry a landing party or to fight at sea. They would fight at sea by drawing alongside each other's ships and attacking each other's crews. Homer has no occasion to mention either of those operations. The ship builders left a space of around 1m undecked along both sides to give the rowers headroom and to avoid the danger of them being trapped below deck at a boarding party's mercy.

What is apparent in the "modern" version is lack of focus. One cannot tell what the main point of the paragraph is nor what is the important element in any sentence. Above all, it is rhythmically dead, whilst the original version is rhythmically supple and alive. The author heard, as well as seeing, what he was writing. And this, more than anything, is what is missing in modern technical, scientific and informational prose.

* page 142 of Constable edition

Incidentally, the *rendition* is also longer! So much for the vulgar view that "modern" English is more concise, precise, *etc.*, *etc.*, whereas "old" English was all long-winded, flowery, *etc.*, *etc.*

Again, it is symptomatic that the computer finds nothing to object to, grammatically, in the latter version whilst questioning "This change was accompanied by another" and the entirety of the third sentence in the former. Only consider the *impacts* (*i.e.* effect) this sort of thing must have on students, foreigners and, indeed, all those academics, politicians and newsmen, let alone businessmen, who seem to suffer intellectual paralysis when faced by the technological wonders of the modern world!

Well, yes, the language is changing—as it always has; but this facile phrase tends to mask from us that it is only people who can change a language, that without speakers the language ceases to exist. The phrase also fails to recognise that language can be subjected to manipulation. Many of the changes described above are the result of such manipulation; there is an engrained and unquestioning belief in newspaper folk that to cut out a word is a meritorious act ("saves space"—as though the space thus saved were put to any better use!)

Again, changes in a language both reflect and endorse changes in the total culture (this is, perhaps, current reigning theory in Linguistics—although the emphasis on the "endorse" is, at best, muted) but what fails to be perceived is that change also reflects and endorses speakers' (and listeners') understanding of the language itself and of what it is and can be used for—if newspaper writers and editors believe, for example, that *protest against* can be reduced to *protest* without alteration of meaning, then this tells us something about the adequacy both of their grasp of language AND of meaning.

Whether deep grammar (Chomsky's "competence") is innate in human beings (which seems probable) is irrelevant to the question of surface competence, by which I mean something much more than Chomsky's "performance". I mean something that distinguishes a good speaker/writer from a bad one—and, indeed, a good listener/reader from a bad one. A good speaker/writer is in full, but not necessarily conscious, control of the language, and the good—perhaps ideal—listener/reader comprehends fully everything that is in the language (N.B. not necessarily the mind) of the speaker/writer. What is striking about our present culture is that the mature (the grown-ups) imitate the immature (the young); this includes parents copying their children and academics copying their students. This is assiduously fostered by the mass-manipulation industries, of course, for there is money to be made out of it.

I daresay the counter-argument is that most of what I have detailed is no more than a matter of STYLE. This may be so—with many qualifications; but my point would be that stylistic changes can and do lead to changes in the language as a whole. Chaucer's style—or styles—was his language. His style modified English Letters and the entire manner of rendering experience, indeed of experiencing experience. At bottom, one cannot distinguish between style and language. The advertising industry knows this all too well. The current "activities" slogan aimed at disaffected adolescents "You want it You got it" bears out my point, here, all too well.

Many of the changes detailed above seem to me indicative of pidginisation—a simplifying and stripping down of the grammatical and morphological system. And whatever the arguments about the adequacy of pidgins for their speakers, I believe that a person's and a culture's conceptual range—including their moral range—is, not exactly determined, but typified by their linguistic resources. But another point is this: that linguistic change implies extinction (which is why Chaucer and Shakespeare cannot be translated into modern English); in the present case of change in the English Language, what is happening is the rapid extinction of both regional and social dialects. The non-Standard dialects of Britain are being superseded not by Standard British English but by American English.

What one is seeing here, I believe, is not only a manifestation of the wholesale change of our native culture, but an active force (an "agent", in sociologists' jargon). People only copy, imitate or adopt what they perceive as superior or desirable (which may or may not be what is officially held to be so). If they adopt a mockney accent, it is because this, in some respect, elevates them in their own eyes and in the eyes of others they wish to be respected or admired by. And the same applies to the adoption of American usage; that amongst the first to do this are the journalists and media-folk tells one something about their self-image—they are an insecure lot whose greatest dread is of being thought out-of-date. This, if correct, implies that one of the greatest "values" of our present age is to be "up there, with it", whatever *it* is. The past is viewed as dead, and not merely by adolescents; and the future lies in the United States of America (that is, as viewed through the mass media and "entertainment industry"). The leading-role accents heard on our local commercial radio station (Hallam FM) are

Estuary and American; advertising is in R.P. or American; the local accent, if heard at all, is always in a "client", *i.e.* subordinate, role. Yet, judging from car stickers and what is tuned into in local shops, local folk accept this as "their station"—as the announcer tells them to ("Your station of the Stars!").

Another force in linguistic "simplification" (*i.e.* reduction) is the uprooting of people from their place of origin; this is found not only in the movement of refugees and asylum seekers but—and this needs emphasising—in the mass displacement of young people from the family hearth and the local school to universities. That these are never seen as, or at least mentioned as, destructive forces implies either academic blindness or the tyranny of political correctness.

The academic sociologist, anthropologist, linguist-ician, may be forbidden by the rules of his trade to utter normative remarks (everything, of course, is equally interesting and normal to them), but this does not mean that everything that happens in language is "just one of those things", like earthquakes and sun-spots. The feminists and *soi-disant* anti-racists, at least, know that language is NOT just a means of communication but has power over perception and behaviour, that it is, to repeat what I said above, an agent (the Sapir-Whorf Hypothesis, if you like—but the notion antedates those two eminent investigators).

You will observe that I do not mention the linguistic catachreses associated with Disgusted of Tunbridge Wells: split infinitives (but the placing of *not* between *to* and the verb is, nonetheless, something else—"To be or to not be, that's my problem"), sentences ending with a preposition, verbs not in agreement with their subjects; neither do I fume about the "true" meanings of words or about "proper" spellings.

Nonetheless, it is symptomatic of an attachment to mere spellings that when American English is mentioned, the first, and frequently the only, thing people can think of is the spelling *color*. And it is true that even spelling is gravitating towards the American norm; so far, we regularly see: *forever, sometime, anytime* (as adverbs), *whatever* (as in "Whatever happened to . . . ?" (*contra* What ever [has] happened to . . . ?)), *onto, analyze, cooperative, socioeconomic, reuse, skillful, fulfill, installment, extoll, enroll, instill, modeled, swiveled, tranquility, meter* [metre], *jail* (never *gaol* now), *hello* (never *hallo* or *hullo* now—and my computer tells me these are "Not in Dictionary", which is untrue), *thru*. (I first saw *thru* in this country in Whitby Museum on a printed notice in 1988, and, since then, in a comment written by a school-teacher and, next, in a university lecture. Not even Webster's Dictionary accepts it.)

American spelling uses the hyphen only reluctantly and thus it not only has *reuse, reenter, coequal, cooperate, socioeconomic, psychoanalyst,* but also *quick dry paint* [quick-drying paint] and a failure to distinguish between *no-one* and *no one,* between *non-sense* and *nonsense,* between *re-dress* and *redress.* This is, of course, copied in this country; our local Co-op offers "Low Fat Carrot Cake" (which brings to mind the "fungi's" of Sherwood Forest referred to above).

On the matter of capitalisation: public notices now commonly fail to distinguish between lexical and grammatical words; there is an oft-repeated advertisement which reads: "Are You Shamed By Your English?" (*contra* "Are you Shamed by your English?"). This may seem trivial, but it nonetheless demonstrates—ironically enough in the context—a decline in linguistic understanding.

If shibboleths are abrogated, then linguistic meaning-potential is lost; one of their advantages is that they can be broken to make a point. "Me and my wife are disgusted" has quite a different force to "My wife and I are disgusted." Similarly, to deliberately split an infinitive is—or was—to make a deliberate point "Be or to not be" is neither what Hamlet said nor what he meant, but could one find any journalist—or novelist—today who would detect the difference? ("But the board is likely to all resign if that happens . . ."*)

I have spoken only incidentally about lexis because this is volatile and fugitive in a way that structure is not. However, any cursory study of recent changes in this will reveal a consistent, and rapid, replacement of British English by American. This both reflects and reinforces the changes in modes of living (*life-styles*) experienced in this country; and these are irreversible. If one takes, say, a limited field of activity such as shopping, a list can be drawn up to illustrate these changes:

A.E.	B.E.
store	shop
village store	village stores
center / centre	shop / warehouse / depot / stores
a mall	a parade / an arcade
pharmacy	chemist's
butchery	butcher's
barber shop	barber's / hair-dresser's

* *The Observer*, 13.10.02, p. 1. A touch of either LDS or schoolboy English, I suggest—*see above*.

A.E.	B.E
aisle	passage / gangway
checkout	till
can	tin
mix	mixture [in B.E. *a mix* = cement or concrete]
pack	packet / box / clutch / batch / bag / file
muffin	bun / fairy cake [a B.E. *muffin* = muffin]
cookies	biscuits
crackers	cheese biscuits
cereals	breakfast food [this now seems very old-fashioned.]
donut	doughnut
french fries	(thin) chips
chips	crisps
fast food	ready-to-eat food [in A.E., *fast* means only "quick", never as in "fasten".]
food to go	food to take away
free range eggs	eggs from free-ranging hens ["free range eggs" must be pretty far gone!]
store in fridge	keep in fridge
use before . . . [in A.E., food, drink, lawyers, cars, roads, wives and husbands are all *used*; a paper could be written on this alone.]	consume / eat before . . .
used	second-hand
Take a look at . . .	Have a look at . . .
Come In And Look Around	Come in and Look Round
Call (on) . . .	Ring / 'phone . . .
regular	ordinary / standard / medium

A.E.	B.E
king size	extra large
mammoth	giant size(d)
pick 'n' mix	pick & mix
gift wrap	wrapping paper
packaging	wrapping / packing
[plastic] sack *cf.* similar lack of discrimination in A.E. *pack* and *rock*.]	[plastic] bag [a *sack* is a big bag.]
sport socks	sports socks
boxer shorts	boxing shorts / underpants
a suit	*both* a gent's suit *and* a lady's costume
bathroom tissue	toilet (lavatory) paper
tissues	paper handkerchiefs
baby wipes	wet paper hankies
baby buggy	push-chair
ad	advert
custom	patronage
custom built	purpose-made
customer notice	notice to customers / manager's notice
quote(ation)	estimate
finance	hire-purchase
just [£2.99]	only [£2.99]
warranty	guarantee
zero	nought / nil [in B. E., *zero* was used solely for temperature.]
Santa	Father Christmas
Halloween	All Hallows' Eve
Mothers' Day	Mothering Sunday
Drive Thru	(Drive Thro') [never seen because American in origin]
Customer Car Park	Customers' Car Park
Exit	Way Out

What of mere "words and meanings"—those things the layman thinks of when he (or she) thinks of language? Some items that currently demonstrate an extraordinary degree of confusion are:

viable   valid
masterly   masterful

[A.E. fails to distinguish or, rather, lacks *masterly*. In B.E., *masterful* = domineering. The earlier T. S. Eliot essays have *masterful* for *masterly*.]

to prise (off)   to pry
[A.E. lacks *to prise (off)*]

to perpetuate   to perpetrate

[This, one hopes, is a mere schoolboy howler—but, appearing as it has in a broadsheet which finds it necessary to explain the meaning of *to loathe* in its corrections column, and which speaks of the *disestablishment* of the monasteries under Henry VIII and of the *St James* version of the Bible, one has one's doubts.]

to persuade   to convince
[The semantic elision between *to persuade* and *to convince* is not dissimilar to that between *to infer* and *to imply* and *to rent* and *to let*. I can be persuaded without necessarily being convinced.]

to let to hire to rent to loan
[A. E. lacks *to let* and this "gap" has reinforced the confusion typified by the schoolchild's "Can I lend yer ruler?"]

uninterested disinterested lack of interest indifferent

("The very reasons [*sic*] that make Romano-British art attractive today brought it the *disinterest* of early scholars."*)

a rock   a stone
[Palestinians are reported as throwing *rocks* at cars—they must be pretty strong!]

to harm   to hurt   to injure

---

* Jennifer Laing, *Art and Society in Roman Britain*, 1997, p. 1

[see section, above, on nominal semantic categories]
      frustrated   angry
[followed by *at* rather than *by*, *over* or *with*]
      meant   supposed
[Now, even the weather is *meant* to be fine, snowy,
windy, *etc.* (Who can mean it so? God, one *supposes!*) *I
suppose* has been absorbed by *I guess*. Note that there is
no equivalent in A.E. of "I don't suppose that . . . (*ironic
/ deprecatory*)". Indeed, this *tournure nuancée* would
probably be lost on many Americans.]
      house   home
[an example of deliberate manipulation by builders,
estate agents and insurers; *to move home* means, in B.E.,
to go back to where one came from, NOT to move
house.]
at least at most at first at last at the earliest at the latest
[all these locutions may be subsumed by *at least.*]

I suppose it is wiser to laugh when *The Times* tells
us—as it did—of the arrival in this country of the
Emperor of Japan and his *Concert*, and, again, when
we read of *slithers* of bombs bursting over Afghanistan,
but when Mark Steyn writes in *The Sunday Telegraph*:
". . . those Europeans . . . evidently feel no *compunction*
to demand from Chairman Arafat any . . . pause for Pass-
over," is one to suppose he knows what he is saying—
and what he means? As for the difference between
persuade and *convince* or *perpetrate* and *perpetuate*, well,
now, that really is expecting too much!

(*The Guardian* complains of stereotypes being
perpetrated against [*sic*] Muslims.*)

It is a curious thing that, notwithstanding all the
multifarious changes overtaking the language that I
have described, yet the old prejudices and snobberies
remain. Thus, northern accents are still held in

* 19.06.02

derision—even, be it noted, by northerners themselves; all south-eastern accents are regarded by northerners as "superior", even those which, in the south-east itself, are viewed as lower-class. This means that /bɑːθ/ is "better" than /baθ/ even though the former might elicit an apologetic giggle. Likewise, /wɔːʔə/ is acceptable amongst the "educated" whilst /watə/ is not. It is not unusual to overhear local speakers—especially girls—guying traditional speech; indeed, I have myself been subjected to this. Everyone simply *knows*, don't they, that local speech is comic; they haven't been taught to think so by the media, oh no no no. One's social superiors will be seen as "affected", especially when beyond climbing reach, but it is only one's inferiors who can be guilty of Bad English. So whatever the social class we aspire to says, that, *ipso facto*, must be correct—and, of course, better than what one's parents, whom one hopes to leave behind, said. Again, it is only one's (unattainable) social superiors who are guilty of snobbery, never oneself. I have encountered, since coming to Sheffield in the '60s, the most outrageous and offensive snobbery from locals who assumed that I, like them, must know without misdoubtings that all regionalisms were laughable; they wished, especially, to feel superior to their own parents—and, in the case of girls, their boyfriends, too, if these were local.

The current slogan for Sheffield Wednesday reads: "Wednesday 'til [*sic* reversed apostrophe] I die"; traditional Yorkshire would say: "Wednesday *while* I die" and write: "Wednesday until I Die". In its little way that sums it up, I think—the destruction of regional cultures as well as the national culture. And, of course, this is both represented in and confirmed by dress, food, leisure patterns and sexual mores.

The whole psycho-sociological question of who (the computer tells me this should be *whom*), in a society, is permitted to question whom about his/her language is of some interest, I think. For instance, I have frequently both observed and experienced jeering attitudes—even in public—to traditional British linguistic forms, but never, since the '50s, to an Americanism or the adoption by a native Britisher of an American accent. It is also the case that one can, here in the Sheffield area, overhear younger females especially making scoring points about others' dialect forms. I have had curious teaching experiences where students have manifested intense discomfort over being faced with some of the—simpler—examples given in this letter, declaring, for instance, that they hate Americans, on the perverse supposition that the intention was to *teach* them American. Perhaps one might invoke that dangerous concept, ideology, here.

The overarching rule of an ideology is that one is not to question its rules or, indeed, to notice that it has any rules. One of the great rules of our ideology is the unquestioning acceptance of change, which is always typified as "progress". Furthermore, it is an un-challenged rule that the direction of this progress is known; anything which does not lie in this direction is typified as reactionary. Thus, we all *know* that language changes; change is a *good thing* and is, furthermore, *proof* of vigour; therefore the language is in a vigorous state. Q.E.D. It is also against the rules to ask what is meant by "language", for, of course, everyone already knows.

One final point: I find that when I make any representation to those responsible for, say, presentations to the public, concerning the accuracy, quality or correctness of the English, there is apparent a total lack of concern. When, once, I attempted to draw the attention of a young curator in a museum to the seven or so faults in the captions in her display, she declined so much as to look, saying that they had been passed by the "Education Department". When, once, I tried to alert, privately, a university lecturer to certain errors in his lectures (*e.g.* pronouncing *detritus* as /diːtrɪəs/ confusing ***procession*** with ***precession*** [of the equinoxes] —and similar matters), the response was entirely self-justificatory. And what is one to say of a learned society which hopes to *instigate* a lectureship? I had no reply from its president when I wrote to him to suggest that *institute* was the required word. There remain, also, those unhappy refugees of the Holocaust who were either *interned* or *interred*—who will ever know which?

YOURS &c.

MICHAEL WALLERSTEIN